BY
FAITH

THE STORY OF
KING'S
GARDEN

BY
FAITH

THE STORY OF
KING'S
GARDEN

MIKE AND VIVIAN MARTIN

ISBN 1-57921-275-1
Library of Congress Catalog Card Number: 99-69285

Mike and Vivian Martin on the steps of the administration building.

Contents

I Live By Faith

Contents

Accomplished By Faith

PREFACE

Mike and Vivian Martin walked by faith, exhibiting trust and confidence in the Lord to use and bless them beyond their wildest imagination and the Lord did exactly that. King's Garden (which became CRISTA Ministries) is the fulfillment of God's promise to answer prayer, showing great and mighty things which we know not. My prayer is that we will continue this adventure of faith, seeing God's hand of direction and blessing which results in changed lives for eternity. All of the glory goes to God for what He has done and will continue to do at CRISTA. Psalm 115:1 states, "Not unto us O Lord, but unto thy name give glory." I thank the Lord for the vision and ministry of Mike and Vivian Martin.

Jim Gwinn, President
CRISTA Ministries

INTRODUCTION

CRISTA Ministries began under the name of King's Incorporated. The original corporation papers were written in 1948 and the organization began its formal activities in the deserted Firland Tuberculosis Sanitorium in 1949, under the name "King's Garden." I moved onto the campus with my parents in 1949 and my formative years were spent on the beautiful King's Garden campus. I graduated from King's High School in 1955.

The two books contained herein were written many years ago by my dad and mom, Mike and Vivian Martin. I often joke that the best decision I ever made was to be born to such godly and wonderful people. Mom and dad had a rather unusual relationship in those days, in that their marriage and ministry was a complete partnership. Mother served as dad's confidential secretary. Very little that went on in the early days did not involve both of them, and all decisions were made after praying together. Dad was the founder of King's Garden and died in 1961. Mother died in 1993 in the Nursing Center at CRISTA Senior Community.

Today there are ten major divisions of CRISTA doing the work of education and compassion in the Pacific Northwest and throughout the world. I know my parents would be thrilled to know I now serve as Superintendent of King's Schools and as a Vice President of CRISTA.

These stories of years ago not only give a sense of the miraculous past King's Garden, but also are relevant for today. They will inspire those who seek to follow Christ.

Tribute needs to be made to the many wonderful people who came out to this place in the early days to work for only $30 per month (plus room and board). Through them the dream of King's Garden became reality. To the King's Garden Old Timers this 50th Anniversary book is dedicated.

I would like to express my appreciation to those who gave their resources to fund the reprinting of these books. I thank Moody Press for the release of the original copyright. Several people deserve credit for doing the work that made this reprinting possible: Kevin Tate, Marvella Berg, Pauline Johnston, Lynda Toben, and Marlene McCurley. Of these wonderful colleagues and friends, the bulk of the effort was done by Marlene who perceived the value of recapturing these two historical and inspiring books at the time of the 50th Anniversary of CRISTA.

S. Michael Martin
November, 1999

I Live By Faith

Introduction
I Live By Faith

Today the world is wondering, "Can God?" We read of the miracles performed by Peter and Paul recorded in the Bible; we read about such men of God as George Mueller and others, and then we wistfully wish that God were still doing the same miracles today. It is not that we doubt that God *can*, but rather we doubt whether in this day God is willing, or we may think that His promises are for another age. Yet we read in Hebrews 13:8, "Jesus Christ, the same yesterday, and today, and forever," but still down deep in most of our hearts we find a doubt. We pray for certain things. Our prayers are not answered. Why? Has God lost His power? Are all of His promises just for the saints of old? Why do we not experience miracles as they did?

The fault does not lie in God but in us. "Oh, ye of little faith." His promises are true. God cannot lie. "If we believe not, yet he abideth faithful: he cannot deny himself'" (II Timothy 2:13). If we meet His conditions, God is still bound to fulfill His part. Today, as of old, literally thousands of miracles are happening. God is today healing the sick, providing money, and controlling the weather in response to prayer. People are living and working full time for the Lord without physical means of support. We choose to call this "living by faith."

This book is written that you, too, may know the conditions necessary to see miracles performed in your own life. Rejoice in the fact that we can claim His promises literally. The miracles and facts related in this book are taken from actual events which happened in the life and among the family and friends of the writer. We can say with emphasis, "Jesus Christ is the same yesterday, and today, and forever." Praise God, it is true!

CHAPTER I

I Heard the Voice of the Lord

I have heard the voice of the Lord audibly two times in my life. The first time was when I was saved, and the second time was when He called me into His service. This was the beginning of miracles in my life.

At the age of twenty-seven one of the greatest miracles which has ever happened to me took place and ushered me into a completely new life. At this time I was living in Bellingham, Washington, and was the owner of a fairly prosperous service station. My greatest concern was to make money and to enjoy life. My wife and I gave very little thought to the Lord and none to death and to the life beyond. Our lives consisted of the normal whirl of the average worldly couple—dances, card-playing, smoking, and drinking. At this time we had two children and were fairly well satisfied with ourselves and the life which we lived.

I had been raised in a good home, but not a completely Christian home. Mother was a fine Christian woman, but my father was unsaved. I was baptized as an infant and went to Sunday school faithfully. I attended church as my parents brought me there. I was confirmed at the age of fourteen. At the time of my confirmation I thought that I had graduated into heaven. Now I had attained. It was not necessary any longer for me to go to Sunday school. I could now do the things I would like to do because I had earned my way to heaven. I proceeded to participate in the sins of the world.

I met my wife at the age of twenty on the dance floor. It was love at first sight. Six months from the day I met her, we were married. About one and a half years later, our little girl, Joyce Elaine, was born into our home. The first thing we thought we should do was to have her baptized, and this we did. We attended church occasionally because we felt we should. I even held a church office. Despite this, we ran with a fairly wild crowd. Each week we went to different dances in the northwest part of Washington. This was during the time of prohibition, but there were still many bootleggers around, and most people attending dances in my crowd felt they had to have beer, wine, or moonshine in order for them to have a good time. In order for us to keep up with the crowd, I participated in the same way. I did not enjoy drinking, but I felt it was the fashionable thing to do; therefore I would proceed to get intoxicated along with the rest. Invariably the morning after I would say, "Never again. I will not drink any more." But over and over again, I went through the same procedure with the same crowd each week. Occasionally when we had sobering thoughts, my wife and I would look at one another and talk about things of the Lord, and many times I would ask my wife, "Viv, do you think if I should die I would go to heaven?"

Immediately her response was, "Sure, haven't we been baptized and confirmed? We belong to the church. What else is there for us to do? I am sure we will get to heaven."

In the back of my mind, however, there was the sobering thought, "If I would die tonight, would I really go to heaven?"

Each Saturday night we went out with the same crowd, first to get some beer, wine, or moonshine and then to go to some dance. On a certain Saturday night, our party bought some moonshine as usual, but this time it was poisonous. Little did I know that some moonshine that was sold had caused people to become blind and that others even became paralyzed. This moonshine did not taste any different—it all tasted bad, but when I wakened on Sunday morning I didn't feel so good, so I stayed in bed trying to recover enough to be able to work on Monday morning. However, I was unable to go to work on Monday and felt even worse than I did on Sunday.

My wife doctored me up the best she could and then left the bedroom. Shortly after she left I had one of the strangest experiences I have ever had in my life. I felt myself becoming weaker and weaker, and then all of a sudden I came to the realization that I could not move my hands or feet. This, of course, alarmed me, and I thought I had better call for help. I then discovered I had lost complete control of my voice and could not speak. I was completely paralyzed. I will never forget that dreadful feeling of utter helplessness and fear which gripped my heart. For the first time in my life I realized what real sickness was, and I became afraid. Understanding my serious situation, I began to pray. Although unable to move my lips, I was able to pray mentally. As I was praying, there came to me a vision of my Aunt Emily who had passed away sometime before. She was a Christian woman, and I knew she had prayed much for me. As I saw her standing by me, I said, "Aunt Emily, aren't you dead?"

She answered, "Yes, I am, but you will be shortly." She then disappeared, and if ever I prayed fervently, it was at that time when the fear of death engulfed me.

I now realized for the first time I was lost and headed for hell. All I could think of was to pray, "Lord, save me. Lord, save me!" At that time I was thinking of being saved physically more than I was of being saved spiritually, because I did not know exactly what it meant to be saved spiritually. Even as I cried out these words inaudibly, the Lord heard that desperate cry.

It was then that I heard audibly the voice of the Lord. He called me by my Christian name and said, "Alvin, if I save you, what will you do about it?" I did not have to ask who was speaking to me. I knew it was the Lord. His voice was a voice of majestic authority.

I cried out, "Lord, if you will save me, I promise to serve you the balance of my life." I had no sooner said these words than the Lord touched my paralyzed body and saved my soul. I knew immediately that I was headed for heaven.

I got out of bed, much excited, my hair disheveled, and dashed into the living room where my wife was sitting at the sewing machine. When she saw me and heard my excited voice calling, "Viv, I'm saved, I'm saved," she became frightened and thought I had lost my mind. She ran out of the house. I ran after her and caught her in front of our neighbor's house, still in my pajamas, crying, "Viv, I'm saved, I'm saved." It took some time before she realized that I was rational, that God had healed me, and something wonderful had happened to me which I could not explain to her even though I tried.

My first thought was, "I must tell Mother, since she is a Christian. Surely she will understand what has happened to me." I got dressed as quickly as I could and got into my Model T Ford and drove down to Mother's. I loved my mother and did not want her ever to know that I often got drunk. Therefore, I decided that I would not tell her that I got paralyzed from drinking poisonous moonshine, but rather I would just tell her the most important thing—that God had saved me.

Mother and Dad operated a three story rooming house, and when I arrived there I ran excitedly up the stairs, crying out, "Mother, I'm saved, I'm saved." Mother was not on this floor, and I continued up the second flight of stairs, still crying out, "Mother, I'm saved, I'm saved." As I arrived on the next floor, I noticed a mop sitting in a bucket of water in the hall, so I knew Mother was near. As I continued to call, she came out from one of the bedrooms, with tears still undried on her cheeks, wondering what I was so excited about. I will never forget that moment as I embraced her and told her I was saved. As we wept together, I tried to explain what had happened to me.

She then told me, "About one hour ago when I was mopping the floor, the Lord told me that something was wrong with you, Alvin. I did not know what it was, but I felt the urgency to stop mopping just where I was, and for the past hour I have been weeping and praying for you, asking the Lord to help you, whatever the trial was you were going through, and above all to save you." God heard my mother's prayer. I believe that I was literally prayed into the kingdom of God by a mother who loved me.

After we had rejoiced for a while, I went back home and again I tried to explain to Viv all that had happened. I still could not tell her how I got saved so that she could understand. All I could think of to say was, "Viv, you have to get the same thing I have." I did not know how to help her but thought if I just could find a revival meeting some place, that's where she could get saved.

About two weeks after this, the Lutheran Church began tent revival meetings. This was what I had been praying for. When I saw the tent and the sawdust trail, I just knew that that was where Viv, too, could get saved. When I took Viv to the revival meeting, she went with the thought in mind of getting saved. I continued to encourage her because I knew Christ was the answer. When the altar call was given, Viv gladly responded, and she and I went forward together. The preacher thought that I came to be saved, too, but I just wanted to help Viv. That night Christ came into my wife's heart. We then and there became a Christian couple, and our home became a Christian home. Drinking, moonshine, and dancing lost their attraction and were forgotten.

After this experience, we tried to tell our friends what had happened to us, but they just could not understand. When they invited us to go dancing with them as before, we refused, endeavoring again to explain that we were saved and would not be going to dances any more. Then one of the men said, "I'm sorry, Mike. I hope you will feel better by Saturday night and can go with us." No matter how we tried to explain, they all thought we were sick or something bad had happened to us. Instead, something wonderful had happened. God had given us a new life. II Corinthians 5:17 became a reality to us both. "Therefore if any man be in Christ, he is a new creature: old things are passed away; behold, all things are become new."

CHAPTER II

God Speaks Again

After our conversion, Vivian and I began to grow spiritually and to serve the Lord. God blessed us and prospered our business until we were selling ten times as much gasoline as when we first purchased our service station. Because of our success, the Richfield Oil Company's representative came to see me one day and asked me to work for them. They offered me an attractive position in charge of over 100 service stations in eastern Washington. My main responsibility was to instruct the service station operators on how to increase their business. Believing that this was a real opportunity for advancement, I took this position. The Lord continued to bless me and gave me advancements with the Richfield Oil Company.

I continued to work for them a few years and then decided to go into the wholesale gasoline business for myself in Goldendale, Washington. We joined the local Baptist church and attended regularly. We taught Sunday school classes, and Viv and I served the Lord in our business.

Our wholesale gasoline business prospered, and we were able to open up two more gasoline plants, one in

Bingin, Washington, and the other in Hood River, Oregon, in addition to the one in Goldendale. We also had some service stations, and everything pointed to the fact of real success and an early retirement in life. In the midst of prosperity I heard the voice of the Lord again.

One night, at approximately two o'clock in the morning, I awakened, feeling very warm and believed I had a fever. The warmth grew until I thought I should wake Viv up to find out what was the matter with me. While I was in the act of reaching over to wake Viv, I heard the voice of the Lord audibly for the second time in my life. Again He called me by my Christian name, "Alvin."

Immediately I knew this was the Lord and I answered, "Yes, Lord."

God spoke in His compassionate, authoritative voice these words, "Time is so short, and there are so many lost." These words broke my heart, and I began to cry. I awakened Viv and told her the Lord had just spoken to me again and had called me into full-time service for Him. She felt my face, and it was so hot she thought I had a high fever. After we talked for a while, I began to cool down, but I was too excited to sleep any more that night. All I could do was pray and praise the Lord. Viv was in a quandary, not knowing what had happened to me.

In the morning I thought I would go to see my pastor, to tell him what had happened and that I believed God had called me into His service. At seven o'clock the next morning I went over to his house. I knocked at the door, and he came to answer. I tried to tell him as best I could what had happened to me in the middle of the night. As I told him I had heard the voice of the Lord audibly say, "Time is so short, and there are so many lost," my pastor looked at me and said, "Mike, I am afraid you had a bad dream. If the Lord had wanted you, He would have called you early in life. He would have called you when you were in high school, and you would have been able to go to college and seminary to prepare for the ministry, but you are a businessman, married, and have three children. You are working for the church, giving money, and you can help supply the finances for someone else."

His words were a tremendous shock to me, but as I continued to listen to him, my faith wavered and I began to think, "This is my minister, a man of God. Surely he must be right. Perhaps I have made a mistake. Maybe after all it was a dream and not the Lord who talked to me."

I came home disheartened, not knowing what to do. I told my wife what the pastor had said and she replied, "It seems logical that the Lord wouldn't want us. We have been working so hard to earn what we have and to make a success in life and we now can. Besides we have our children to rear. You are not a preacher."

I listened to my pastor and my wife and began to feel I had made a mistake. I became ashamed and did not tell anyone else of this experience for a whole year.

From that moment on I had no joy or happiness in my heart. Where before the Lord had been prospering us, now everything was going wrong in the wholesale gasoline business. The Second World War started, and we had to close the bulk plant in Oregon. It seemed everything went wrong.

One day in November, one year from this experience with the Lord, I decided to take Vivian with me because I was going to make a gasoline delivery to friends of ours, Mr. and Mrs. Clinton Groves. Vivian visited with Lottie Belle, Clinton's wife, while I made the delivery and talked with Clinton. After I had finished the delivery, Lottie Belle invited Clinton and me to come in and have some coffee and cake. While we were eating, I began to tell about the experience I had had one year before when God had spoken to me. I told them everything, including my visit to the pastor and his telling me I had had a bad dream. As Lottie Belle listened, she said, "Mike, you made a big mistake. That was the Lord."

As she said that, the fear grew in my heart that perhaps I had missed the will of the Lord. I asked them if they would kneel and pray with me to ask the Lord if this was really His call and if it was, that He would get me out of business. As we knelt together around the table at the Groves' farm, the Spirit of God came into the room as we cried out to the Lord. I remember praying, "Lord, if this was really you who called me, get me out of business."

The Lord heard our prayers. In two weeks a man purchased our business. I was afraid, not knowing what to do or where to turn. However, both Viv and I now had the full assurance that the Lord had called me. Now I was heeding this call and going out into His service.

CHAPTER III

My New Life Begins

"For promotion cometh neither from the east, nor from the west, nor from the south. But God is the judge: he putteth down one, and setteth up another."
Psalm 75:6,7

If anyone had told me that I would some day be serving the Lord in full time service I would have laughed at him, thinking it was a good joke. But Psalm 75:6 is literally true, and early one morning in November between 2:00 and 2:30, God gave me a real promotion by calling me into His service. He did not ask me how old I was, how much education or money I had, nor whether I was married or single. Rather the Lord called me with a challenge I will never forget, "Time is so short, and there are so many lost." As I enlisted in the army of the Lord, I knew that my responsibility was to obey the Lord and leave consequences to Him.

My family consisted of my wife Vivian and three children: Joyce, 14; Curtis, 9; and Michael, 4. We were a closely knit family who held daily devotions and prayed over our problems together, although we participated in many worldly amusements. I believed it was all right for me to drink a glass of beer or wine, and I smoked two packages of cigarettes a day. I was what might be termed a carnal Christian, but this one thing I knew, I was saved. I had a deed to heaven, based on the Word of God. Romans 10:13: "For whosoever shall call upon the name of the Lord shall be saved." I also knew how the Lord had called me into Christian service.

Up to this time I had never given much thought to studying the Bible. Frankly, to me the Bible was a closed book. The word "Exodus" meant a place of exit, not one of the books of the Bible. I knew that if I was to be able to help anyone else, I first must know more of the Bible myself. That meant Bible school, and to start to school at the age of 37—well, ordinarily that was just not done. As I prayed for guidance, I knew that was what the Lord wanted me to do, so with a timid heart I left Goldendale, Washington, alone, seeking the Bible school the Lord would have me attend.

I discovered that any decision made for the Lord is also challenged by the Devil. When I arrived in Portland, Oregon, I visited the petroleum company with which I had been connected. I was ashamed to tell them that God had called me into His service, so I told them I had sold my business. Thinking that I would be looking for new work, they offered me a very lucrative position in the petroleum transportation field. In this position I would have control, both in hiring and firing, as well as in operations. It was a position which naturally anyone would desire. The Devil stood on one side and said, "Now you can really do these things you have longed to do: have money, retire early in life. Then you can give money to the Lord. You're too old anyway to start school now." I began to waver, looking back to what I had done, wondering afresh if it was really the Lord who had called me. I began to think, "God wouldn't want a fellow like me, anyway. I have had no college education; I never have made a study of the Bible, and besides, I have three children and a wife to support." The more I reasoned, the more logical it became that I should take this position.

I'll never forget sitting there in that luxurious office and saying to those who had offered me the position, "I'd like to have a few days to think it over. I have been thinking of going to work for my Father." I never told them I meant my heavenly Father. (Still ashamed! Romans 1:16 was still not a reality in my heart.)

In the meantime I continued to seek for the Bible school I should attend. Somehow I expected that the minute I had entered the right Bible school the Lord would say, "This is the school." Instead of this I became confused after visiting several schools. I looked around and saw that practically every student was in the late teens or early twenties. What would people think of me. My family and friends, other than my wife and the Groves, still did not know why I had sold out my business. I knew that almost everyone would think that somehow or other, Mike Martin had gone overboard on religion, possibly was a little "teched." I could see them wagging their heads, saying, "Too bad, and he had such a good start." Oh, I'll tell you the Devil knows all the arguments. When you step out to serve the Lord, beware. Don't listen to the Devil's so called logical arguments. Invariably two or three doors will open up at the same time, but only one door is the door of God's choice, the others are second best.

By the time I arrived in Seattle, I was feeling pretty blue and disgusted. I took the bus to my Uncle Marion's home. I started afresh to visit other Bible schools, eagerly expecting to hear God's voice saying, "Mike, this is the school," but nothing happened. I began to think, "Has God forgotten me?" For two cents I would have gone back to Portland and taken that job. "Woe is me." I had done everything except the right thing. I had looked and run to and fro in vain. I was all worn out trying to find out what I should do, but I hadn't stopped long enough to pray effective prayers. I became desperate.

Almost a week had passed and I was worse off than when I began but, thank God, I turned to the Lord in prayer. I spent practically all night seeking His guidance. That night I learned a great lesson. The greatest time saver of all is prayer. If I had only gone to the Lord earlier in prayer. Of course I had prayed "catnap" prayers, but I mean prevailing prayer where you hold on to God until you have His answer. I would have saved myself much agony and concern.

Having spent most of the night in prayer, along towards morning I came to the conclusion that I might as well go back home to Goldendale. I gave up trying to find out what school I should attend and told the Lord I had tried, and now if He wanted me to go to Bible school, He would have to show me where. I must admit I felt quite defeated in the morning. Being low in spirit,

My New Life Begins

I thought, "What will my wife and children think of me?" I had left home with such high hopes, confident the Lord had called me and would direct me to the right school, and now here I was going back home a confused, defeated man. As my mind wandered I thought of the position I had been offered in Portland, my call to the Lord's service, and of my home and family. I determined not to let my family know how downhearted I felt. In looking at myself in the mirror, I noticed that even my appearance was downcast. Therefore I decided to have my hair cut and my shoes shined and at least make my appearance neat so that when I arrived back at Goldendale my wife would not see my despair immediately. In many ways I felt the Lord had forsaken me. In this condition I started for the bus line, intending to go to the city center to get myself spruced up.

As I walked towards the bus line, deep in thought, I suddenly became aware that I had passed a barber shop a short distance back. My mind began to function again and I thought, "Why go all the way to town when here is a barber shop right at hand?" I turned around and walked back and slumped into the barber chair. As is the custom of most barbers, this one began to talk, carrying on a more or less one-sided conversation. I was too occupied with my own thoughts to pay much attention to what he was saying.

All of a sudden my mind became alert. What was this? The barber was talking about the very thing with which I was concerned. The words I was hearing came rolling out as if they were instruction from the Lord Himself. The words were about like this: "You know,

35

if I was a young man like you (here I was 36 years old), I would go to a Bible school and prepare myself for the Lord's service. Now you take me. I am too old, but I have been making a study of the splendid Bible schools on the coast. There are many fine schools, but the one I would go to is right here in Seattle. It is called Simpson Bible School. It was founded by A. B. Simpson, the man who also founded the Christian and Missionary Alliance Church and missionary work." As I sat there, spellbound, I realized this: God was guiding me. My prayers of that night had not been in vain. God was using this barber to tell me my next move.

When I had recovered from my astonishment, I told the barber, "I came in here just for a haircut, but instead the Lord sent me here for His instructions." I then explained to him how the Lord had called me and how I had looked in vain for a Bible school to attend. Indecision and doubt left me. I rushed over to Simpson Bible School to see the Rev. Fred Hawley, the Registrar, to make my application as a student.

I will never forget our conversation as I told Mr. Hawley, "The Lord has told me I am supposed to enter Simpson Bible School. I smoke, I drink a little beer and wine, but I know that God has called me. If you will let me come, I know the Lord will take my smoking and drinking away before I register." I am so thankful Mr. Hawley accepted me on this condition, and he told me he, too, believed that God would take these filthy habits from me.

CHAPTER IV

God Performs Another Miracle

The first problem before me was to find a place to live. While in Seattle I stayed with my uncle, Marion Martin, who was a real estate man. I therefore assumed it would be easy for him to find a house for me to rent. Seattle is a big city with many manufacturing plants, including Boeing Airplane Company, and many shipyards, mills, and other large industries. Because of the Second World War industrial boom, Seattle's population almost doubled. I soon discovered there were no houses available for rent. My uncle did the best he could, but the cheapest home he found for me to rent was $100 a month. That, of course, was prohibitive, considering the expense of going to school and the cost of food and clothing, which was high during war time. I would not be able to go to school at that rate.

By this time I had learned that nothing is impossible with God, so I turned to Him again, praying, "Lord, I need a home to live in, partially furnished, at a price cheap enough for me to afford, and large enough for my family of five."

The next Sunday I attended church and there asked if anyone knew of a house I could rent. At the close of the service, the minister told me he had heard of a home for rent in the Green Lake district, near the Bible school. I secured the name of the owner, a Mrs. Nichols, and when I returned from church, I phoned her to inquire about the house.

When Mrs. Nichols answered the phone, I asked her if she still had her home for rent. She laughed and said, "Oh, no, I've had my home rented for about four months. The people who have been living in my place had to move to California, but new people are moving in next week, after I have had a chance to finish fixing the place up. These new people made arrangements to rent my place four months ago when they heard that my renters were moving to California." We talked together a few minutes more, then regretfully I hung up the receiver.

That night as I prayed before going to bed, it seemed to me that the Lord kept saying, "That is your new home," while my thoughts kept going back to the words of Mrs. Nichols, "Oh, no, my home has been rented for about four months." Naturally it was foolish for me to consider Mrs. Nichols' home. I hadn't seen it, and I didn't know if it would be desirable, but still the Lord continued to speak to me, "That is your new home." Finally I told the Lord that in spite of the fact that the place was rented, I would go over and see it early in the morning, and that if He wanted me to have that place, He would have to go before me and do a real miracle. I then had complete peace and drifted off to sleep.

The next morning at 8:00 I was knocking at the door of Mrs. Nichols' home. Evidently she had intended to "sleep in" this morning, for after I had rung the bell, I waited quite a while before a sleepy, white haired lady opened the door, with a questioning look on her face. I greeted her with a smile and asked, "Are you Mrs. Nichols?"

"Yes," was the answer.

"My name is Mike Martin. I am sorry to have awakened you, but I am the one who called you on the phone last night to inquire if your place was for rent."

Whereupon Mrs. Nichols interrupted with, "I'm sorry. Evidently you misunderstood me last night. This home has already been rented. I've had it rented for approximately four months, and the people are moving in next Monday."

We were still standing at the door, and I could see that she was beginning to get cold. As I spoke to her I had a prayer on my lips, "Lord, help me." I began again: "I know that, Mrs. Nichols, but I am a Christian and last night I prayed much about finding a place to live in Seattle. It seemed as if the Lord kept saying, 'This is your home,' so I just had to come down and see and talk with you."

By this time Mrs. Nichols was quite chilled. She could see that I might prove hard to get rid of, so she invited me in. She said, "I, too, am a Christian, Mr. Martin; so also are the people to whom I have rented the house. They have been living in a two room apartment with another family for a long time; they have been waiting for the past four months to move in here. So you can see that it is impossible for me to rent to you. I'm sorry."

I told Mrs. Nichols about the Lord calling me into His full-time service, and that He had directed me to Simpson Bible School to prepare to serve Him. While I was talking, she began showing me the entire house. It was just what we needed—three bedrooms, partially furnished, the right location, and above all, priced at a figure we could afford. I could still hear the Lord saying, "This is your new home."

At the same time I was listening to Mrs. Nichols saying, "I don't know why I am showing you this house. As a Christian I can't go back on my word to these other people who have been waiting for so long for this house."

I said, "I know that is true, Mrs. Nichols, but somehow I can't get away from the fact that I believe the Lord has told me that this is my new home, and I believe God is going to work it out somehow." After a few minutes of conversation I got ready to go, but before leaving I told her that I was leaving for Goldendale that noon and if anything happened that the other people decided not to rent the house, to call me before noon at my uncle's place. She smiled, but nevertheless took my uncle's phone number and promised to call me if anything of that sort happened.

As I walked back to my uncle's home, the Lord began to assure me I was in the center of His will. Before I arrived there, I was convinced I was going to live in that house. In fact, I was so sure of it that I told my Uncle Marion I had rented a house. He was surprised and asked me all about it. I am sure if I had told him the particulars, he would have thought it just wishful thinking on my part. However, the scripture, "According to your faith be it unto you," was a reality in my heart. I was sure that I had heard from the Lord. I sat down and wrote out a check to Mrs. Nichols. Then I told my uncle, "Mrs. Nichols will call you up, possibly after I have left, and tell you that I can have her home. I wish that you would take this check for the rent and tell her that you have the check and will send it to her." My uncle readily agreed and I made arrangements to leave on the noon train for Goldendale. I bade them good-by and started down the street to catch a bus. I had just crossed the street when I heard Uncle Marion shouting for me to come back, I had a telephone call.

Who do you think was there? Yes, it was Mrs. Nichols. The minute I said, "Hello," her voice came excitedly over the phone. "You know, Mr. Martin, the strangest thing just happened. You remember the people who had rented my home? Well, the wife just talked to me on the phone and said she dreamed about you, Mr. Martin. She said the Lord talked to her in the dream and told her some-one was coming to rent their home, and that she should give it up for them. When I told her all about you, she said to get in touch with you immediately and rent the house to you."

I then told her that since the Lord had already prom-ised me her home to live in, I had already made out the check to her for the first month's rent. Praise the Lord for His faithfulness. He will speak even in dreams and in other ways to perform His will. I have never had the plea-sure of meeting the lady who had this dream, but I do know that the Lord some day will reward her for her prompt obedience.

CHAPTER V

Looking for Work

My new life of serving the Lord was just beginning. The miracles which I had already experienced were only forerunners of those which were to come. My wife and I discovered a new checking account in a bank that never fails, as we began to bank on the Word of God.

It was hard to step out from the business world and leave our many friends. As we left Goldendale, very few people understood us. Most of those we knew thought we had gone overboard on Christianity. They said, "Imagine a fellow leaving a good business to start to school at his age. How does he plan to support his family?" To tell you the truth, my family and I were scared as we stepped out, but one thing I was sure of was that *the Lord had called us out.* He had called us out of our business, and therefore we believed that He also took on Himself the responsibility of seeing that we had a place to sleep and eat and the necessities of life. Jesus said, "Seek ye first the kingdom of God, and his righteousness; and all these things shall be added unto you."

We arrived in Seattle on December 12, 1942. After unpacking, we spent Christmas with my folks in

Bellingham, and then came back to begin our new life. My family and I had a business meeting to analyze the way to proceed. We came to the conclusion that my wife and I should both work. At this time work was plentiful. In fact, almost every firm of any size was hiring anyone who applied.

The Bible says, "Be careful (anxious) for nothing; but in everything by prayer and supplication with thanksgiving let your requests be made known unto God. And the peace of God, which passeth all understanding, shall keep your hearts and minds through Christ Jesus" (Philippians 4:6, 7). This lesson I had to learn the hard way. It was not that I didn't want to pray to the Lord and ask Him for the right work, but rather with work so plentiful I felt I didn't want to waste the Lord's time in asking Him for something I could take care of myself.

We started out separately looking for work, confident we would find positions immediately. Evidently my wife had committed her way to the Lord because that evening when we came home, she had obtained work as a stenographer, while I had looked in vain. The next day again I spent in fruitless search.

The following day I went to an employment office. Looking on the large blackboard where work of all kinds was listed along with the amount of money paid for each job, I selected the best paying job which I felt I could handle and made my application. After a lengthy wait and filling out a number of forms, I was accepted and sent out to the place where I was to work. I presented my work slip, and the office girl called the personnel man. He picked up my work slip and read it with a puzzled look. "I can't understand this," he said. "I have all the men I can use and I have not sent notice to the employment office for any more. I'm sorry, but perhaps later you can try us again." I tried to talk him into giving me a job anyway, but soon saw it was useless. I left there a bewildered, discouraged man.

The Lord had many lessons for me. I felt really disappointed that night. Here I was—a strong, healthy man, and the papers were full of ads for men to work, yet I couldn't find a job. That night my wife and I talked over the day's activities and came to the conclusion that we had approached the problem of my work the wrong way. Therefore we prayed together and first asked the Lord to forgive us for not consulting Him, and then asked for guidance. Then the Lord led us to be more specific with Him. He asked, "What kind of work do you want? What hours do you want? What pay do you need?" Before I had not been specific with the Lord. I had been praying, "Lord, guide me to find a job," while He wanted me to state just what I wanted.

Through this experience I discovered that this principle goes for anything we desire of the Lord. Instead of just praying for souls, I think we should pray, calling them by name whenever possible. If we need money, we should pray for the specific amount we need and tell the Lord what we need it for, and, praise God, He answers! By being specific with the Lord, I have found He is specific with me. I have found out that the Lord's will is usually good common sense, mixed with prayer. The adage, "Pray as though it all depends on the Lord and work as though it all depends on you," is surely true.

These first lessons on prayer were put to definite use right then and there. I humbly asked the Lord for work during the hours I had free. It sounded impossible. I knew that shortly I would be going to school and that I would not be able to work all day, and possibly there might be afternoon classes. This would make it hard to have any established hours unless it would be night work. I knew that it would be impossible for me to work nights, go to school all day, and do well in my subjects, so I came to the conclusion I needed a job where I could work during any hours I had free. For example, on the days I had only morning classes, I could go to work at 1:00 P.M.; other days when I had afternoon classes, I could not go to work until 3:00 or 4:00. To go to an employer and say, "I want work, but I can't work any 'regular' hours," seemed impossible. Nevertheless that was the kind of a job I needed, and I asked the Lord for it. I also asked the Lord humbly, but boldly, for work fairly close to both my home and school. I resolved to leave my work completely in the Lord's hands and prayed to be guided where I should go to find this kind of a job.

I waited two or three days before I saw an ad which seemed right, both in remuneration and location. As I prayed about this ad, I believed that the Lord told me to apply for this job. The opening was with a large tire company which specialized in retreading tires. I was more or less acquainted with that type of work, in as much as I had been in the gasoline and tire business.

I well remember the afternoon I went down to apply for this job. Several men were applying for the same work, but only two or three would be needed. It looked rather hopeless with so many applying and with the handicap of irregular hours I had to offer. The man hiring the help, I discovered, was prejudiced against my religious faith and, therefore, it was with a trembling heart that I went in for my interview. I was very frank with the manager. I told him I had been called by the Lord and that I was enrolling in Bible school. Then I dropped the bombshell that I could only work certain hours and those hours to be chosen by me each day. Immediately the manager said, "That is impossible. What kind of an organization would we have if each man worked like that?" I explained to him as best I could that I had been praying for the Lord to guide me, and that I felt this was the place. He was very kind, but said he didn't see how this could be possible. He said he would let me know in a couple of days. Normally this could only mean I was not hired.

I went home disappointed, feeling as though the Lord had forsaken me. I waited two days and then called up the tire company, asking if it had been decided who was to be hired. The manager merely stated that he had my phone number and that if he wanted me, he would call me.

I continued to pray for work. Still I could not get rid of the idea that this tire company was the place I was supposed to work. That the Lord was guiding me was proved two days later when the manager called me to come down.

"I don't know why I am doing a thing like this," he told me. "It sounds foolish to hire a man and let him work whatever hours he wants to, but it sounds interesting. It will make a good experiment. I'll take a chance and we will see how it turns out."

Praise the Lord! He can change the heart of man. His wonders never cease!

The work at the tire company proved a blessing all the time I went to school and until the Lord launched me out on ever greater missions of trusting Him also for my livelihood. All told, I worked for the company two and one half years. There were over 100 employees, and I was the only one who came and went at will, working different hours practically every day. Some days I went to work at 3:00 in the afternoon, working until 6:00, or again, perhaps until 10:00 or 11:00 at night. As the tire company was open 24 hours a day, I even went to work as early as 3:00 A.M. on a few occasions. I never missed a day, except by choice. My work was pleasant. Only the gracious Lord Himself could guide me to this kind of situation! Despite my somewhat weak faith, when I asked Him for work where I could choose my own hours, I learned that it is just as the Bible says in Matthew 13:58, "And He (Jesus) did not many mighty works there because of their unbelief." This verse has been true in my own life, too. Many times I covenanted with the Lord to stay with the tire company until He moved me, which I did.

Now that I had a good job, I still had one more big hurdle before I could start to school, and that was my smoking habit. Mr. Hawley had accepted me on the condition that I no longer smoked. I had tried to quit many times, and each time I had failed. I had smoked for 18 years, and I now was smoking two packages of cigarettes a day.

After I had been saved, I continued to smoke for a few years and had no convictions about it until one night when my family and I attended a Free Methodist revival meeting. During the time of announcements, about half-way through the service, I went outside the tent to have a cigarette. A man who was standing outside, came up to me and asked me if I was a Christian. I, of course, immediately said, "Yes."

Then he said, "If I was a Christian I wouldn't smoke."

I got so mad at the man and thought, "What right has he got to tell me what to do?" That was the first time the conviction hit me that the Lord wanted me to quit smoking. Up to this time I know that it was not a sin for me to smoke, but from that moment on, every time I smoked a cigarette, I felt guilty and convicted about it, knowing it was against the Lord's will for me to smoke. Therefore, I believe it was a sin to me to smoke from that time on. The Bible says in James 4:17, "Therefore to him that knoweth to do good, and doeth it not, to him it is sin." I know this is true. There may be something that today I allow myself to do without sin that tomorrow will become sin because God tells me it is against His will for me to do it. Anything contrary to His will that I continue doing is, I believe, a sin for me. I now measure my habits by asking if the Lord would do this or that. If He would, then I can. I am sure He would not smoke; therefore, I will not smoke.

Some people have told me that when they became Christians they quit the smoking habit immediately, with no struggle. It seems that I do everything the hard way. I am so thankful though that the Lord has patience with me. I tried a number of cigarette cures with no luck. I even tried rolling my own, mixing in with the tobacco things I did not like, but still there was no victory. I would pray and resolve over and over again, "This is the last cigarette package I will ever buy. Just as soon as I finish this one, I will quit." I would sometimes throw away my cigarette pack, carefully noting where I had thrown it away, then going back later trying to find it. The cigarette habit really had me for over 18 years. I could not quit in my own strength, but now I was up against it. I knew Simpson Bible School would not allow me to enter if I continued to smoke. I had given my word to Mr. Hawley. I had come to the end of my rope. I literally gave up trying and told the Lord, "Lord, you know I have tried in every way I know to overcome this filthy habit, but I just can't. Lord, unless you come to my rescue, I am sunk. You know I have told Simpson Bible School that I would quit, but I can't. You will have to help me. Please, Lord, take this bad habit away from me."

When I knew I could not do it in my own strength and surrendered to Him, God undertook, and I was delivered from this habit. Where I formerly carried my cigarettes, I now carried a small New Testament. Because of the habit of many years, I would reach there occasionally for a cigarette, but instead I would feel the New Testament, and God gave me strength as I felt His Word there. I have been so thankful and praise God for this victory, and that Mr. Hawley accepted me as a student, believing that God was able and would deliver me.

CHAPTER VI

God's Saturday Nights

After I had worked two weeks, the winter term for Simpson Bible School opened. With fear and trembling I started to school. Most of the students were in their late teens, a few in their twenties. I felt like an old man and I was, in the opinion of the majority of the students. I was as old as most of the teachers and older than some. It was almost 20 years since I had been in high school. I was sure I had forgotten all I had ever learned, and for a few days it seemed I really had.

It took quite a while to adjust myself to my new role as a student. Memorization was almost impossible for me. I remember some of the spelldowns we had for Bible memorization. I soon discovered that I knew practically nothing of the Bible. Standing with these youngsters who rattled verses of Scripture, I felt foolish, as I always went down on the first verse the teacher gave me. I remember how hard some of the teachers tried to help me by giving me a choice of verses, even saying most of the words with me, as I stood there dumb and embarrassed, finally sitting down in defeat. The only verses I knew were John 3:16 and Psalm 23.

After a time things began to be easier. I began to learn. Gradually the Bible opened up to me in a new way, and life became dynamic and meaningful as I brought my school work to the Lord. I learned how to study. My schedule was quite full, with going to school in the morning and part of the afternoon, working at the tire company most evenings until ten o'clock, then getting up early in the morning to study before going to school again.

My free time was from Saturday evening to Monday morning. I found that one can get so busy doing the legitimate things that he does not take time enough to get alone with God, to read His Word, to pray, and to give service. As a student going to Bible school, it was necessary to read almost daily in the Bible for certain assignments, but I soon discovered that it was also absolutely necessary to read the Bible voluntarily to feed my own soul. Reading the Bible as an assignment is fine, but the joy of just sitting, reading, and letting the Bible search your heart does something for your soul that nothing else can do. It took me quite a while to learn this because with all my work and school life, it just seemed there was not enough time to get alone with the Lord.

I had thought when I got to a Christian school it would be so easy to be holy. Surely everyone there would be a Christian, loving everyone else. To my surprise I found out that the Devil works everywhere. The sheltered life among Bible students makes Christianity almost commonplace. Someone has said that it is harder to stay on fire for the Lord in a Christian school than any other place. In many ways that is true, because Satan tries to lull you to sleep.

Without realizing it, I began to lose my first love. I heard the Word given by competent teachers every day. At first I was sitting and drinking in all the wonderful truths, but I became as a stagnant pool, with an inlet but no outlet. It was approximately six months before I realized my condition. Then I began to seek the Lord afresh, spending time alone with Him.

I promised I would give Him every Saturday evening for Christian service. I remember the first Saturday night, as I went out of the door, my wife asked me what service I was going to. I told her I didn't know, but I had promised the Lord I would give Him this night, and I knew He would direct my path. I had a few tracts and a New Testament with me and although I was afraid, I was determined to serve Him. I was still afraid to go up to someone and start talking to him about the Lord.

There was still pride. What would people think of me if I handed out tracts on the street corner? I started for Skid Row, believing it would be easier there, and besides none of my friends would see me. Before arriving there, while still in the main part of Seattle, I saw a street meeting. I stopped and listened as five or six young people played musical instruments, sang, and gave testimonies.

The Lord began to speak to me, telling me to get out there with them. I was panic stricken. What if my uncle or others that knew me came by? "Lord, I will do anything, but please not a street meeting." Excuses raced through my mind, but there was no argument against that still, small voice from God saying to me, "Go out there and stand with them." Finally, obedient and with shaking legs, I stepped into the street and stood by the side of one of the young men. He looked questioningly at me, but I said nothing. He handed me a songbook, and I soon was trying to blend my voice with theirs.

The leader then came over and asked me if I would give a word of testimony for the Lord. I nodded in agreement, and it was with mingled emotions that I began to speak. I started in a loud but faltering voice to say that I knew Jesus Christ as my personal Savior. After a sentence or two I felt my throat muscles closing up. My voice became husky, then froggy, and then began to leave me. I floundered to a stop, and the leader to cover my predicament, started singing a song. I had made a failure of my very first assignment.

I made up my mind to stay away from street meetings in the future. The next Saturday night I still faced my promise that I would give the Lord every Saturday night. This time I was determined not to go to the street meeting but to Skid Row. But my feet found their way to that same street meeting. God would not let me go any other place, so I determined I was going to give a real testimony for the Lord this night. The group started in the usual manner with songs and special numbers, and in a little while a number of people were stopping to listen. Soon the leader asked for testimonies. My heart beat faster by the minute as I realized he would soon call on me, which he did. There I stood again before the street microphone. I just wasn't going to make a fool of myself this week. I would give a clear, clean cut testimony if it killed me. "I am so glad I am saved," I started to speak out in a loud voice. But immediately my voice began to leave me again. I tried desperately to clear my throat. The second and the third time I tried, but a silly squeak was all I could muster. My lips were moving, but the words wouldn't come. Again the leader came to my rescue and announced another song. Disheartened and more scared than ever, I wondered how I could ever be of any use to the Lord. Nevertheless the urge was still in my heart. The promise I had made to God to serve Him every Saturday night still stood.

The following week I went to school as usual, studying hard and going to work afternoons and evenings. Finally Saturday night arrived again. This time I had practiced what I was going to say. I felt in my heart I would not fail again. Again we met for prayer, and again I was at the microphone. This time I was more bold when I began to speak, but after a few words the same trouble faced me. My throat began to close. The words would not come out. I was an utter failure. I don't know how the leader felt, but I know how grateful I was when he announced another song. After the meeting that night, as I prayed, I felt that the Lord was showing me that this was not my main ministry, but rather a place of training. However, as He hadn't shown me any other ministry or opened any other door, the following Saturday night found me again on the street corner.

The leader did not ask me to come out and stand with the group, and I didn't blame him. My mind was churning. How *could* I serve the Lord if I couldn't talk like the others did? The crowd on the street corner was small that night. Nearly everyone hurried past, some with indifference, some with open scorn. I longed to persuade them to stop and listen, to hear words of life. Suddenly on an impulse, I reached out and took the hands of some Christians who were also standing on the corner. We stood in the middle of the walk holding hands so that no one could get by. Soon there was a large crowd. People had to stop because we blocked the way. Others going by and seeing the crowd, became curious and stopped, too. In a few minutes we had the largest crowd we had ever had, and people were listening to the testimonies of the fellows who could talk! The Bible tells of being a doorkeeper, but I guess I was one of His first road blocks. I was really happy. I had found something I could do, even if I couldn't speak. This was another lesson for me. I realized that if one is determined and eager to serve the Lord, not caring about personal pride, there is always something one can do. The Lord has a way of guiding us when we take our hands off of our own lives.

My adventures with the Lord on Saturday nights now really began. The street work was just a beginning of launching out on greater and greater thrills in serving Him. For a while on Saturday nights my primary work was personally talking with those individuals who became interested, pointing out scripture verses, dealing with their problems, and witnessing to others, person to person, endeavoring to win them for Christ.

One of the assignments I had facing me at the Bible school, that I dreaded, was speaking in the school chapel before the whole student body and faculty. Every student was required to do this, and since I knew I could not escape it, I decided to give my personal testimony of how the Lord saved me. I knew I could never preach a sermon, but with the Lord's help I determined to do my best. Finally came the day, and with trembling legs I stood and told how the Lord saved me out of a life of sin. At the conclusion of my personal testimony, a pastor who sat in the audience came up to talk with me and asked me to speak at his church the following Sunday. I immediately said, "No. I am sorry. I can't speak. I have never preached a sermon in my life. I am not ready yet." I thought this was the only proper thing to do. I was thinking only of my own weakness, completely disregarding the power of God to use a willing person.

A short time later, I was talking about this with the Rev. Henry Turnidge, a pastor friend of mine, telling him laughingly, "Can you imagine what happened? A pastor asked me to speak in his church."

"Did you take it?" he asked.

"Of course not. I've never preached a sermon in my life."

He did not laugh with me as I expected, but said, "Mike, you made a bad mistake there. You should go in every door the Lord opens for you. If you don't go through the open doors, He will not open up others for you." I have found that this is the method the Lord has used to guide me into new work for Him. Almost invariably the Lord gives me jobs that are beyond me, but He helps me. When I fail, the experience drives me to my knees, and in that position I learn faster. "*From here on, Mike, take every assignment* the Lord gives, until you get so busy you have to make a choice."

I was so thankful to Mr. Turnidge for this counsel. From that time on, I have tried to follow this advice, with the exception of times when I was physically unable to speak or had to make a choice between two or more opportunities for service. I resolved to say "Yes" to my next invitation to speak. A short time after this lesson I received a call from one of the missions in Skid Row, asking me to speak. I accepted the invitation and started to walk into the doors the Lord opened for me.

I will never forget the night I stood on the platform at Peniel Mission, ready to preach my first sermon. My legs shook, and I shook all over. I was glad there was a pulpit for me to hang on to. Without it, I am afraid I would not have been able to stand. I had so much in my heart that I wanted to bring these people—how Jesus was born, how He was raised, about His sufferings, crucifixion and resurrection, and that He had done all this for me. I began by reading the Scriptures telling of Jesus dying on the Cross. I became so engrossed in what I was saying, all my notes were forgotten. I started out with the virgin birth of Jesus, and there was so much to say about that wonderful event in the Lord's life on earth, I didn't get beyond His life at the age of twelve. Since I took all the time telling of His childhood, I never had time to tell of Jesus on the Cross. For this reason the sermon and the Scripture didn't tie up very well together. My wife was in the audience, and she was very concerned and felt sorry for me as she listened to my stumbling words and thought, "Mike will never make it. I know he will never make a preacher." (I believe she was right in this.) Certainly I used no homiletics that night, but the Lord used me anyway, for when I gave the invitation, a number of men came to the altar. I discovered that it was not so much what I said, but if my heart was clean before the Lord, then the Holy Spirit could take my stumbling words and accomplish His ends. The Lord gave me love and compassion for these unfortunate people as I talked to them. Vivian was no more surprised than I was to see men come forward after a message given so poorly, but praise the Lord, "God hath chosen the foolish things of the world to confound the wise; and God hath chosen the weak things of the world to confound the things which are mighty; and base things of the world, and things which are despised, hath God chosen" (I Cor. 1:27, 28).

This experience at the Peniel Mission was the first of several opportunities I had to speak there. The Lord used this mission to help train me. Needless to say, I spoke in fear each time. Even to this day it is a fearful thing for me to stand behind the pulpit to give out the Word of God.

On one occasion when I spoke at Peniel Mission, at the close of the service a young girl came forward and knelt at the altar and cried out to God. We talked with her, and she told us her story. She had run away from her home in Montana the day before, and on the bus a strange man had made her acquaintance. He was with her, walking on Skid Row this night, and as she walked by the Peniel Mission street meeting, she felt the urge to go into the meeting. Her new acquaintance tried to hinder her, even pulling her away as she came in, but she persisted. During the meeting he left her, but entered two or three times and tried to get the girl to leave with him, making quite a disturbance. When I gave the invitation to those who would like to accept the Lord, she came forward and accepted Christ as her own personal Savior. After hearing her story, we had the police pick up the man waiting outside. They discovered that the man was a white slave dealer who, if God had not intervened, would have taken this girl for his evil business. He had promised to help her secure employment and show her Seattle. Undoubtedly this girl had someone praying for her that saved her from a life of sin and sent her to the mission that night where she found Christ. The next day she returned to her home in Montana, and the white slave trader was sent to jail.

Another time I will never forget at the Peniel Mission was a night when at my invitation many men came forward for salvation. I noticed one man especially who had been drinking heavily, beginning to weep at the altar. I knelt by him and put my arm around him. As he cried out to the Lord, I saw the Lord make him completely sober and transform this drunkard into a saint. Later as I walked out with him at the close of the meeting, I was telling him of the necessity of reading the Bible daily, praying, and telling others he was a Christian, and that he would have to leave this old life of the Skid Row and sin. As we walked together, one of his buddies came staggering up, waving a bottle and saying, "Come on, Bob, let's have another drink." I stepped up to the man and said, "Bob just got saved."

Then Bob himself spoke up and said, "No, Jim, I'm not going to drink anymore. I just got saved."

Whereupon Jim grabbed Bob saying, "Aw, come on. Just one more drink won't hurt you," and began to literally pull Bob away from me.

I pulled on the other side, shouting, "Let go of him, Jim. What you need is the same thing as Bob has."

Jim quit pulling on Bob and said, "I am too great a sinner to be saved."

I then repeated for him Isaiah 1:18, "Come now, and let us reason together, saith the Lord: though your sins be as scarlet, they shall be as white as snow; though they be red like crimson, they shall be as wool," and then I said, "Jim have you ever killed a man?" I was intending to conclude my sentence that God would even forgive a murderer, but I did not get a chance because Jim let go of Bob and ran like greased lightning down the street. I then realized I had been talking to a murderer. What must that man face on the day of judgment without Christ?

I am so thankful to God for the opportunities He gave me to preach on Skid Row. The Lord blessed me and gave me souls every time I spoke there.

CHAPTER VII

The Beginning of King's Teens

Many of the experiences the Lord led us into were precious and served as a pattern in miniature for our future services at the King's Garden. Our first September in Seattle, the Lord began to guide us into our future work of helping boys and girls from broken homes. One night Joyce mentioned at the supper table that Joanne Paping, a girl she knew at school, had asked to live with us. Joanne was a new acquaintance of Joyce's at school, and we had seen her only once or twice. Our immediate reaction and reply to Joyce was, "No, Joyce, we do not have enough money." Surely, we thought, there are other places she can go, and people who know her better than we do who can help her. So the next morning at school Joyce told Joanne that we could not take her, and we thought the matter was closed.

The next day the Lord began to speak to both Viv and me and reminded us that we had promised to obey Him, and that we hadn't even prayed about Joanne's coming to live with us. We talked together, prayed, and asked His forgiveness, and we told the Lord if *He* wanted us to take Joanne, to have her come the second time and ask Joyce if she could live with us. If she came again with this request, we would know that God was sending Joanne to us.

The very next day Joanne again saw Joyce at school and asked if she please couldn't come to live with us, at least for a while. That evening when Joyce told us this, we knew the Lord was sending Joanne, and we told Joyce to bring her home the next evening. How we praise the Lord that we were obedient in this, for just two days later Viv had the joy of telling Joanne about Christ, and the same night Joanne accepted the Lord as her personal Savior.

Joanne had been to church only once or twice in her life and then to a church where the Gospel was not preached. Slowly but surely now, there came a change in Joanne. The things of the world began to fall away, and she began to enjoy her new life of going to church, young people's meetings, and other Christian activities. II Corinthians 5:17 began to be a reality, "If any man be in Christ he is a new creature . . ."

There were times, however, when it was quite difficult both for her and for us. Her temperament and former environment were so different from ours, and we knew little of her background. All Joanne had formerly known was uncertainty and fear. When she first came to live with us, upon going to bed at night, she would start trembling and waiting, expecting Viv and me to begin fighting and quarreling, which she had been accustomed to hearing in her own home. However, God was faithful and helped both her and us in the time of adjustment. Little did we know that Joanne was the first of hundreds of teenage boys and girls from broken homes that we have been able to take in and assist at King's Garden. I believe that if we had not taken Joanne in the Lord would not have given us the opportunity of helping others, nor would He have given us King's Garden.

One day Joyce came home from school, disheartened and blue. When we inquired the reason, she told us, "Everything is arranged for those who are not Christians at school. All the parties are either for dancing or other worldly amusements that Christians cannot approve. I wish someone would do something for the Christian kids."

The Lord used this remark to burden my heart for the Christian boys and girls in high school. I started to pray that the Lord would put it upon someone's heart to work with these teenage boys and girls. I had prayed for some time along this line when the Lord began asking me to do something about it. I tried to explain to the Lord that I had never worked with young people. I couldn't sing; I couldn't speak; I couldn't direct music. But all these arguments were in vain. The Lord began dealing with me, telling me He wanted me—not someone else—to work with high school boys and girls. It seems that every step along the way I have tried to get others to do the work He has wanted me to do. However, when the Lord reminded me that I had promised to obey Him, I surrendered my will to Him again and told the Lord I would be willing, but that He would have to show me what to do.

I started working with John Lundberg soon after that. Johnny already had a work going for high school boys and girls. He was a gifted singer, a very fine young people's leader, a director of music, and a good speaker. As I worked with him I felt less qualified than ever, but I determined to go on.

One day as I was praying I told the Lord that any time He had any word for me or any instructions, if He would awaken me between two and two thirty in the morning, I would know it was He. Of course He has spoken to me at other times, but it has been my custom for a long time, that whenever I awaken at night between two and two thirty I get up and meet the Lord in Bible reading, meditation, and prayer. The Lord has used this time for instructing and guiding me in most of my important spiritual decisions and challenges which have affected not only my life, but the lives of many others.

A few weeks after this, the Lord wakened me early one morning and began to speak to me. He gave me the name "The King's" and asked me to start a new teen age work. That night on my knees King's Teens was born. He gave me the pattern which we are now using in King's Teens interdenominational high school club work. The main emphasis of King's Teens is to get the Christian teenager going for the Lord and to give him Christian fellowship in school. Over and over again we see teenagers making decisions for Christ, but what happens the next day and the day after? King's Teens was raised of God to help that Christian teenager, to encourage him to testify, study the Word, join and work in the church, and to reach out and win for Christ those in school who would never otherwise hear the Gospel. Our motto is "obedience to the Word of God."

The Beginning of King's Teens

I intended to start our first King's Teens Club in our home and began to plan for this when to our surprise Mrs. Nichols, our landlady, came and told us her son and his two children were coming home to live with her and therefore she would have to ask us to find another place to live. We were amazed and heartsick and began to ask the Lord, "Why did this have to happen, when we were so comfortable and getting along so well?" It was impossible to find a place to rent, we soon discovered, so we began to think of the possibilities of our finding a place to buy. By this time we had spent our money, and we had almost nothing to use as a down payment. We knew that unless the Lord undertook we would be in bad straits.

One day I happened to mention to Bill Ellison, a clean-cut high school boy who was working with me at the tire company, that we needed a home and asked him if he knew of a place we could rent or buy. To my surprise he said his dad had bought a place but since his mother didn't like it, they were planning to sell it and buy another. Bill introduced me to his father, Major Ellison of the Salvation Army. He took me out to see the home and as I looked at it I felt in my heart that it was ideal for my family. It was within three blocks of the Bible school I was attending; it had a large living room for King's Teens meetings and it reminded me much of the home I was raised in. A few days later I secured the key from Major Ellison and took my family to see the place. They, too, were pleased with the house, and when we began to pray together, we believed this was the house the Lord would have us purchase.

Major Ellison told us he had to have $1,900 in cash in order to get his investment out. The Major and I prayed together about the house, and he told me that he felt the Lord would have us purchase his house. He gave us a thirty-day option to give us a chance to secure the money. At this time we had no money at all, and we tried to figure out ways and means. We sold our car, which netted us money for part of the down payment, but we still lacked more than a thousand dollars. I also endeavored to find someone who would be willing to take a second mortgage on the house. We tried everything, but at the end of thirty days, the money was still as far away as ever.

I went back to see Major Ellison and told him that we did not yet have the money, but we still believed the place should be ours. While I was in his office he had a call from a real estate man, offering more money for the house than the price made to us. But Major Ellison turned it down to allow us more time to raise the money. He told the real estate people to wait another week and then if we couldn't get the money, he would sell to them. He then told me he still felt the Lord wanted us to have the place and that he would wait just one more week. If on the following Monday at twelve o'clock noon we did not yet have the money, he would have to sell to the other people.

I remember how we tried to borrow and even tried to pawn my wife's diamond ring. We prayed much that week, but every door seemed closed. I made one last appointment Monday morning in the office of the Graham Investment Company. Before I left for the appointment, our family prayed together, and my oldest boy, Curtis, said he felt sure the Lord was going to give us that place. He was the only one who still seemed to have the faith to believe. All of us had believed so confidently at the start, but when every door closed and the last day had arrived, our faith was greatly diminished.

At approximately 10:30 A.M. I went to the Graham Investment Company and met the man who had been considering loaning us the money. However, he said their company could not loan the money to us on a second mortgage because of FHA restrictions on older homes. As I heard him say this, it took the spirit out of me, but I felt I should give him my testimony anyway. I told him that I was a Christian and that God had called me out of business and told me to combat juvenile delinquency through Christianity. I also told him that my family and I believed that the Lord was going to give us this house, but that evidently the Lord had other plans for us because I knew He could have delivered the place if it had been His will.

After this gentleman left the real estate office, Mr. Graham, a fine Christian man who had been sitting quietly and listening, came to me and said, "I listened to your testimony and I have confidence that the Lord wants you to have that house. Just yesterday a man came in and paid me some money which I did not expect, and I believe that the Lord wants me to loan you the money so that you can buy the place." My heart leaped for joy, and I looked up and saw the clock on the wall. It was just a few minutes before noon. The option on our home would be canceled in a few minutes. I asked permission from Mr. Graham to use his phone and called Major Ellison to tell him that the Lord had, at the last minute, given the money. Major Ellison and I praised the Lord together over the phone. How wonderful it was to have our new home sold to us by a Christian man, and the money loaned to us by another Christian man. Surely the Lord was guiding our affairs. It didn't take long until we moved into our new home. The house was partially furnished, and it was wonderful to see that just the items of furniture we needed were included in the furnishings. We had given our piano to the church when we left Goldendale, but there was even a piano waiting for us! Everything fit perfectly. It was such a comfortable place, with three bedrooms upstairs, hardwood floors and a fireplace, full basement and oil furnace. Although it was not a new house, it was perfect for us.

After we were settled, our thoughts began to turn again to the work the Lord had called us to do, that of working with high school boys and girls. We made plans afresh to start our first King's Teens Club, which would meet in our own home. I had the best of intentions, but I always seem to learn the hard way, so instead of starting King's Teens right away, I again started to work with John Lundberg. This was not the Lord's will, and things just did not work out right. There was very little interest. At one meeting there were only four teenagers, and two of them were my own children, and they *had* to come! Things went from bad to worse. Finally in November, 1944, the Lord dealt with me and asked me why I was not following the pattern that He had given me. I asked Him to forgive me, and as I was there on my knees, I began to ask the Lord for the souls of teen age boys and girls. The Lord said to me, "You obey me and do as I say, and I will give you souls." That night through prayer, King's Teens was born the second time. How wonderfully God has blessed! Since that time hundreds upon hundreds, yea, thousands have found Christ, and many other thousands have dedicated their lives for full-time Christian service in King's Teens Club meetings. This would not have happened except for an experience that happened to me the night of November 14, 1944.

CHAPTER VIII

The Holy Spirit

Simpson Bible School began each school day with a chapel service, usually with Gospel singing, a special musical number, and a speaker. I will never forget those mornings as I sat in the chapel and listened to speaker after speaker talk about the Holy Spirit. This was something new to me. I was not acquainted with this kind of preaching. Yes, I knew I had received the Holy Spirit when I was saved; His Spirit witnessed with my spirit that I was a child of God. But when I heard them speak of men such as D. L. Moody, Charles Finney, A. B. Simpson, and other men of God, my heart became hungry to be like them, and I desired that I might be used of God in a greater way. I knew they had the power of God resting on them in a way which I had not experienced. Many of the speakers I heard had something that I knew I needed, which was more power in my life to testify and to win souls for Him. I needed what they were talking about, but I did not know what to do to receive this power. Yes, I was working for God. I was walking in all the light that I had, but I wasn't seeing the souls saved that I felt I should. I spoke, but I lacked something. Then one day as I heard one of these men speaking on Acts 1:8, "But ye shall receive power after that the Holy Ghost is come upon you, and ye shall be witnesses unto me both in Jerusalem, and in all Judea, and in Samaria, and unto the uttermost part of the earth," I whispered a prayer, "That's what I need, God! I need the Holy Spirit to give me this power."

I began to pray daily, asking the Lord that I might receive the Holy Spirit, in order that I might see more souls saved, and that I might be able to see more things accomplished for God. One morning, November 14, God woke me up at 2:00 A.M. As I looked at the clock, I knew this was His time. I went downstairs, not knowing what the Lord would have, for each time was different. Usually I would pray and read the Bible and ask the Lord what He wanted with me. I knew this morning it was something special.

As I knelt at the davenport, I began to pray again, asking the Lord for the Holy Spirit with power that I might win souls for Him. The Lord spoke to my heart and asked me if I really wanted souls. I told Him, "Lord, I do not care what it takes or costs, I must win souls."

Then the Lord began to deal with me. He did not talk audibly, but in that wee small voice that we who know Christ understand, He began to talk to me, saying, "Alvin, will you give me your name and fame?" I noticed that He called me by my name of Alvin, the name given me when I was christened as an infant. Everyone calls me Mike, but I know my name in glory will be Alvin.

As I knelt there, it was so easy for me to say yes to this. Name and fame? I had no name; very few people knew me, and I had no fame. "This is easy," I thought, "if this is all it takes to receive the power of the Holy Spirit." With no hesitation I replied, "Yes, Lord, you can have my name and fame." I didn't think I was giving Him anything. I didn't realize how pride can come in subtly and a man can begin to boast of that which God does as though it were His own doing and rob God of His glory.

I waited anxiously to see what the Lord was going to do or say next. Soon I heard the Lord say again, "Alvin, will you give me your home?"

My wife and I had already dedicated our home to the Lord, but this was different. I knew now that the Lord wanted the house literally, so that if He should ask us to sell it and move into a tent and give the money to Him that would be all right with us. This really wasn't too hard, though, because Viv and I truly had already committed our home to Him. That night though I had to give the house to Him afresh, saying, "This house is completely Yours, Lord; You can do with it whatever You wish."

As soon as I made this commitment, I believed that the Lord would then fill me with His precious Spirit. I waited before the Lord, but nothing happened for a long time. Then I heard again, "Alvin, will you give me your boy, Michael?" This startled me. Michael was our youngest boy, our baby. I couldn't quite believe that God would want to take him away from us. As God continued to talk to me I soon believed that He really wanted him to be taken home to heaven.

I cried, "Oh, God, let me keep him and I will raise him for You."

But all I could hear was, "Will you give me Michael?" I continued to weep and tried to reason with the Lord, but I got no answer except, "How much do you want souls? Will you give me Michael?"

Finally after wrestling with the Lord, I came to the place where I could surrender. I thought, "At least I have two children left; I still have Curtis and Joyce."

I said, "Yes, Lord, You can have Michael." I prayed and waited, again believing that I would receive the Holy Spirit, but not knowing exactly what to expect.

Again I heard the voice of the Lord, "Alvin, will you give me Curtis?"

Again I wept. I remembered the time when Curtis almost died of pneumonia. A minister came and anointed him with oil and prayed for him, according to James 5:14, 15. We dedicated him to the Lord that night in the hospital room and said, "Lord, if You will spare our boy, we will raise him for Your service." I know the Lord heard that prayer because He healed our boy. I reminded the Lord that Curtis was already His, that He had been dedicated to Him. However, I knew this time that the Lord was not just talking of dedication. He wanted Curtis completely and I felt sure it meant Curtis' death even as Abraham offered up Isaac. I wept and cried to the Lord and finally He gave me grace to lay Curtis, too, on the altar for Him. I knew that if I wanted to see souls born again, I had to surrender him, too, as a living sacrifice.

I reasoned that surely now the Lord would not require more. "At least I have my girl left; I have Joyce."

After some time I heard that wee, small voice talking to me again, saying, "Alvin, will you give me Joyce?"

Again I tried to reason with the Lord and asked Him if I could not keep just one of my children so that I might have the joy of raising one for Him. I loved my children and I tried to explain to Him that if I could just keep Joyce it would be bearable.

But all I could hear was, "Do you want souls?"

I knew I had to give up my girl if I wanted God's best. As I gave Him Joyce, I was sure it meant her death, too. "If any man come to me, and hate not his father, and mother, and wife, and children, and brethren, and sisters, yea, and his own life also, he cannot be my disciple. And whosoever doth not bear his cross, and come after me, cannot be my disciple" (Luke 14:26, 27). This scripture became a reality to me. I waited again, expecting the Holy Spirit to be given now. Also I began to see that Luke 14:33 was what God expected of me. "So likewise, whosoever he be of you that forsaketh not all that he has, he cannot be my disciple."

Again I heard the voice of God speak to me. "Alvin, will you give me your wife, Vivian?" This was a tremendous shock to me.

I cried, "Lord, I have to have a wife if I am going to serve You. I need a wife to help me. Please let me keep Vivian." I alternately cried and prayed, trying to explain to the Lord my need of a good wife.

All I could hear Him say in return was, "Alvin, will you give me Vivian?"

After crying and praying for some time, I finally was able to say, "If this is the choice I must make and You need the whole family, I will choose You, Lord."

I then went upstairs—it was now five o'clock in the morning—to say good-by to my family, as I expected them all to die in just a little while. I first knelt by the bedside of Michael and said, "Good-by, Michael, my boy." I laid my hands on him and kissed him as I wept, and said, "Lord, here he is, your boy Michael."

I then went over to Curtis, laid my hands on him, kissed him, and said, "Good-by, Curtis. I know I will see you in heaven . . . Lord, here is your boy, Curtis."

Next I went to Joyce's bed, laid my hand on her, kissed her, and said, "Good-by, Joyce. See you in glory . . . Lord here is my sacrifice."

The children continued to sleep, little knowing that I expected them all to die in a few minutes.

Last of all I went in to Vivian, still crying, woke her up, and excitedly said, "Viv, you are going to die in a few minutes." She was startled, awakening out of a sound sleep and wondering what it was all about. I tried to explain, with tears running down my cheeks, that in a little while she was going to die. She couldn't understand it, but I remember kissing her good-by, thinking I was seeing her for the last time alive.

Finally I went downstairs and knelt by the davenport and sobbed out, "Lord, You now have everything." I then had an experience I will never forget. It seemed as though heaven itself opened and I saw the glory of the Lord. I cannot explain it. All I know is that I felt I was in the presence of the King of kings in a pool of liquid sunshine. The glory of His presence was so strong I could not stand it and finally had to say, "Lord, I cannot stand it," and His glory lifted slowly. I do not know exactly what happened, but I do know that I was anointed by the Holy Spirit with power, for after that I preached many of the same sermons I had preached before, but now with a new authority and power, and I saw many souls born again. Ever since this experience, God has continued to bless me in a remarkable way, and many people have found Christ as their personal Savior through my ministry. I know that Acts 1:8 is a reality, that I have received from Him the Holy Spirit with power.

I believe receiving the Holy Spirit is not just a once and for all experience, but we need a fresh infilling of the Holy Spirit from day to day. I find that I need a daily infilling for each task He gives me to do. Although this crisis experience changed my life, I know that it is necessary for me to feed daily on the Living Bread and receive from the Lord a new, fresh anointing of the Holy Spirit for each day's work. Little did I know that besides the King's Teens Clubs, He had in store for me King's Garden and many other affiliate works.

I know the things He has done through my life have not been by my power, but by the power of the Holy Spirit working in and through me. This time in my life was precious as it helped me know Him better. I know now by actual experience Luke 14:26 and 33. God does demand a complete surrender of everything—name, fame, houses, lands, wife, and family—everything to be His true disciple and to be used of Him.

I Live By Faith

The Lord has been so good to me. I had expected Him to take my complete family home to glory immediately, but instead He has allowed me the privilege of keeping them all. Joyce is now a missionary in New Guinea, Curtis is a minister of the Gospel, Michael is in school preparing to go to the foreign lands as a missionary if the Lord so leads, and Joanne, the first girl the Lord gave us from a broken home, is a minister's wife. My wife and I are now grandpa and grandma, serving the Lord together at King's Garden. Although we are wonderfully blessed, my family and everything is still on the altar. We are all His and He can do with us whatever He desires.

CHAPTER IX

King's Teens Work Expands

After my experience of November 14, the work of the King's Teens took on new life. With a beginning of only four teenagers (two of them my own who had to come), we were soon crowding out our living room. Each week there were from 80 to 100 teenagers coming to our home. There was a great deal of enthusiasm in the group, and every week there were boys and girls who gave their hearts to the Lord. How wonderful it was to see their lives changed! We could feel and see the Spirit of God working with these youngsters. Our neighbors could hear the singing two blocks away. I could visualize the shingles on our roof flapping up and down trying to keep time with the youngsters as they sang with all their might. Some of the harmony might not have been the best, but it was loud and enthusiastic and, above all, something was happening in the hearts of the teenagers.

As I look back to the beginning of King's Teens, I remember how I argued with the Lord when He told me to start working with teenagers. I tried to explain to Him that I could not sing, let alone lead the singing, speak, or do anything, but the Lord reminded me that when He called me, He did not call me because I had any talents. He did not ask me how old I was; He did not ask me how much education I had! He did not even ask if I was married or if I had any children. He just said, "I want you to come and serve me." I am so thankful that He did. I know my responsibility is to obey the Lord and then leave the consequences with Him. When I completely surrendered, I became an empty channel which He could use. I gave Him my mental and physical faculties, and He took over.

The first meeting of King's Teens was most difficult for me. Not knowing how to direct music, I just stood before the young people trying to make them sing, not moving my hands but just standing still and urging them to sing. I had a low voice and could hardly carry a tune and there I stood, shouting, "Sing." You can imagine how miserable the singing was. My wife said one day, "Mike, you have to do something besides just saying, 'Sing.' Wave your hands, stamp your feet, clap your hands, but do something."

Not knowing what else to do, I began to tap my foot, trying to keep time with the music. Finally I became so enthusiastic with the singing that everyone around could hear my foot beating, "thump, thump," even over the loud singing.

Again my wife (bless her dear heart) said, "Mike, you have to do something besides stamping your foot. You are going to knock a hole right through the floor."

So again I prayed, "Lord, help me," and I began to wave my hands like I had seen song leaders do. I have never been able to do this in quite the right way but, praise God, I now can lead young people so that they will sing. When I obeyed the Lord in this, He gave me a new singing voice. My voice actually came up one whole octave higher so that I was able to sing along with the teenagers and sing loud enough for them to follow. I will never be a soloist, but I can now make the kids sing and enjoy it.

With more and more teenagers coming, my wife and I needed help. We began to pray, and the Lord sent Joe Brill and, shortly thereafter, Jim Thompson, students from Simpson Bible School. Joe and Jim led the singing and helped with the counseling work. With many more girls coming, we began to pray for another woman, and the Lord sent Miss Janet Theodore (now Mrs. Normand Hutchinson) to help.

We began to have inquiries about King's Teens, and people began asking us if we would start a club in their neighborhood. Our first call came from Cephas Ramquist, a businessman from Vashon Island, near Seattle. Mr. Ramquist said he was having a weekly meeting for teenagers, but only five or six kids were coming. He asked if we would come and start a King's Teens Club there, which we did. God blessed in a real way at Vashon and soon 30, 40, then 50 were coming each week. Many of these teenagers found Christ as their personal Savior, while the Christian teenagers began to enjoy their Christianity and to win others. We were thankful for this privilege of launching out.

Our third King's Teens Club was started on Bainbridge Island, at the home of Mr. and Mrs. Berg. Again God blessed, and boys and girls came from everywhere on the island, and many found the Lord. God demonstrated that His hand was upon King's Teens, and soon we had clubs throughout the state of Washington. We next expanded King's Teens into the state of Oregon, with Ernest Eells as director and headquarters in Salem, Oregon. We began one of the first clubs in a migrant labor camp in Oregon. None of these boys and girls had ever heard any Gospel songs and choruses. In the middle of the first meeting, all of a sudden they all got up and ran outside. I had no one left in the meeting, so I followed them outside to see why they had left. There in front of our meeting place, I saw a husband beating up his wife. The crowd of adults and teenagers just looked on, and when the episode was over, the boys and girls came back into our meeting. I was shocked as the man knocked his wife to the ground, lifted her up to hit her again and again, but I discovered in talking to the young people that this was a common, everyday experience. I listened as they told me some of the squalid conditions of their lives. Most of them never attended school. Their parents forced them to work, picking up potatoes in the fields. They stayed in one place just until the school truant officers would catch up with them and force them to put the children in school. The parents would then move on to some other place again, putting their children to work. It seemed to me that all they were doing was using the children for earning money, so that they could get drunk. In many of these labor camps the young people were not supervised, and in one instance some teenagers took two small children and put them into an oven and actually roasted them alive.

When I first asked the camp manager if we could come in and provide some recreation and a club meeting for the kids, he said, "It would not work. We tried it once." Upon inquiring, we discovered that they had given the kids a building, a slot machine, and a piano with no one to supervise them. The kids spent their money on the slot machines, then later at night they broke into the building and ripped the machine to pieces trying to get their money out, and in their anger did other damage to the piano and building. That was the end of the recreation. I thank God that through King's Teens we were able to reach a number of these boys and girls for Christ. God continued to bless, and soon we were able to see King's Teens expand into other states also.

King's Teens Clubs normally operate only during the school year, from September through May, so that I had the summers free to prepare materials for the opening of the clubs in the fall. During the first summer after starting King's Teens, I received a call from Lake Sammamish Bible Camp, asking if I would come out for two weeks to serve as counselor in their boys' camp. I eagerly accepted the offer, as I had promised the Lord I would walk into each door He opened. I went to my employer at the tire company and requested my vacation so that I could serve the Lord for these two weeks at Lake Sammamish Bible Camp. He granted me this, as I had a vacation coming. The Lord blessed the boys' camp in a marvelous way.

Two weeks later, Dr. and Mrs. Annis Jepson, directors of boys' and girls' camps at Lake Sammamish, asked if I would come back again for their next boys' camp. I had no more vacation time coming, but I went to my boss anyway and asked him if I could not have an extra week off as I had been asked to work for another week at Lake Sammamish Boys' Camp. He said, "Isn't that just what you did two weeks ago?" I told him it was. After considerable explanation, he reluctantly granted me an extra week away.

Again God blessed in a real way. Shortly after I had returned to work at the tire company, Dr. Jepson called me again and asked if I would come out just one more time for their last camp of the season which was for high school boys and girls. Again I went to my boss to try to secure another week off. This time he said sternly, "Mike, you will have to make a choice. Either you are going to work for me or for the Lord. Which do you choose?"

I had been longing to be out in full-time service for the Lord for some time. I had asked the Lord to thrust me out. This was it, I knew, as I replied to him, "Mr. Brown, this is not a difficult choice for me. I told the Lord a long time ago, 'Lord, when You want me to leave this job and go into full-time service for You, thrust me out so I will know You are doing it.' I have been waiting for this moment for quite a while and am so glad that now I can serve the Lord with all my time." When I finished talking with Mr. Brown, I returned to my work.

As was my custom during the noon hour, I turned the radio dial to listen to the Christian Business Men's program. Hilding Halvarson, Seattle's well-known Gospel singer, who has meant so much in my life, was singing, "God is Waiting." As I listened, I knew the Lord was talking to me through Hilding's song. I spoke audibly, "Lord, you don't have to wait any longer. I am ready to go." After the song had ended, I went downstairs to punch the time clock. The tire company had a bulletin board right by the time clock. As I glanced at the bulletin board, I was startled to see pinned on it a poem entitled, "Get on the Firing Line for Jesus." As I read the poem I thought, "Surely the Lord Himself has pinned that poem on the board just for me!" During the two and a half years I had worked for the tire company, I was the only one who ever had been allowed to put anything of a Christian nature on the bulletin board, and I was permitted to do this only at Christmas, Thanksgiving, and Easter. This, I knew, was God's seal to me. A few minutes before, I had told my boss I was choosing the Lord, then I heard Hilding sing, "God is Waiting," and now this poem, "Get on the Firing Line for Jesus!"

I was never more sure about anything in my life than I was that this was God's time for me. This was truly the beginning of my walk of faith—working for the Lord without any gainful occupation, trusting Him for our bread and butter, for clothing, and for everything we needed.

A simple definition of living by faith is, working for the Lord without any physical means of support, having God take care of all your physical needs such as food, clothing, rent—all of your financial help coming from God through the tithes and offerings of God's people, but not having any guaranteed support. Something new happened also in our new life of "living by faith." We began to see miracles happen in new and strange ways. I had asked the Lord for help in understanding the Word of God and in actually believing it. God began to answer this prayer. I knew that God cannot lie. Then I reasoned if this is true, I had better believe God and act like it. As I began to see this, He gave me faith to walk this new way of life, living by faith.

CHAPTER X

I Live By Faith

As I went out to Lake Sammamish this time, severing all connections with my work at the tire company, I felt I was going all out for the Lord, that I was now actually getting on the firing line for Jesus. The first day of full-time service was quite a thrill to me, and I have never regretted it or lost the joy of trusting Him for my livelihood. The Lord blessed the boys' and girls' camp in a marvelous way. As far as I could ascertain, all the boys and girls at this camp accepted Christ, and I too was blessed in my own heart. I came back home on Saturday evening to see how things were going and discovered that we were in bad shape financially. Viv and I prayed about it, asking the Lord for help as on the following Monday our $50 house payment was due. We had no savings account of any kind. We explained to the Lord our desperate situation and told Him that if He did not undertake we would not have the money to meet the house payment of $50. All we could do was leave this problem in His hands. It was necessary for me to go out again to Lake Sammamish early Sunday morning for the closing meetings.

Each Sunday afternoon there was a special service with emphasis on missionary giving. A missionary was chosen for the week, and the offering was then given to this missionary. The missionary chosen was usually a missionary on furlough from some foreign land. As the meeting progressed, I was thrilled to hear the boys and girls tell about the wonderful things the Lord had done in their hearts; some had found the Lord during the week, and others had dedicated their lives for full-time service.

Now came the climax of the meeting. The big moment was when they announced the missionary of the week. This choice was always kept a secret by the directors, Dr. and Mrs. Annis Jepson, until this big moment. No one knew who it was. It was one of the biggest thrills of my life to hear them announce that the missionary of the week was—guess who?—Mike Martin! What a wonderful way God had chosen to show me I was in His perfect will. As I went forward to receive the gift of the missionary offering, all I could think of was the chorus, "Praise Ye the Lord." With tears of emotion and joy coursing down my cheeks, I just stood there smiling through my tears. Finally I choked out, "Can we sing, 'Praise Ye the Lord'?" As we sang that chorus, my heart went up in thanks to the Lord. I received in that offering $252.57. As my wife and I checked back on what I would have earned during the time I was at camp, we found that the Lord took care of us even better than if I had stayed on the job at the tire company. With this money we were able to make our house payment, put in a supply of groceries, get other necessary things, and even have a little left over.

We had another real thrill after I returned home from my first week of service. Our youngest boy, Michael, was just getting ready to go upstairs to bed one night when he began to cry. He cried as though his heart would break and I went to him, not knowing just what was the matter. I asked him, "What is wrong, Michael, did you hurt yourself?"

He began to sob, "I want to get saved. I want to get saved."

I am so glad the Lord said, "Suffer the little children to come unto me." What a thrill it is to lead your own boy to the Lord! I put my arm around him and said, "Come upstairs and Daddy will pray with you."

We talked together first about what it meant to be saved and when I asked him what had happened, he said, "As I was thinking of going up to bed, I looked on the table and saw the salt and pepper shakers, and it seemed that when I looked at the pepper shaker, I saw the Devil in the shaker and he said, 'Come on, Michael, I want you.' I got scared and looked at the salt shaker and I saw Jesus in the salt shaker, and He said, 'Michael, come to me. I want you.'" Again Michael began to sob, "I want Jesus. I want to get saved."

It was a real privilege to kneel alongside of my boy and hear him cry out to Jesus to save him. Even though Michael was only seven at the time, the Lord truly came into his heart. Michael, as a young man, dedicated his life to the Lord and is now preparing for Christian service. Truly God can speak in strange and miraculous ways to reach the lost.

The work of King's Teens was not yet developed to the point where I could devote my full time to it. As I considered and prayed about this, I felt that the Lord would have me sell Bibles and Christian merchandise during the daytime and work in King's Teens at night. I talked with a man who was in the colportage business, and he helped me get started with Christian greeting cards, birthday cards, and other Christian materials. I was still a little fearful of trusting the Lord all the way. After trying to sell these various Christian items for a few weeks, I came to the conclusion that I should not sell birthday and Christmas cards, etc., but rather just sell Bibles along with the King's Teens work. This gave me a good opportunity to talk with people about their souls at the same time I was demonstrating the Bibles.

As I look in my diary which I kept for a time, I find this notation, "The Lord allowed me to sell three Bibles today, two in homes where they had no Bible. They also allowed me to pray for them." I was able to place many Bibles in homes which did not have one. Each day I asked the Lord for directions, and God blessed in a real way. For the period of almost two years that I sold Bibles, I believe I only missed two or three sales. Every place I demonstrated a Bible, I made a sale. I am not that good a salesman, but the Lord guided me, and I obeyed His orders. A few times I never even demonstrated the Bible, but made the sales while standing on front porches. The Lord really made the sales, and I only took the orders and collected the commission which was at times from

$5.00 to $7.50. One day Viv and I had a special, urgent need for money. The house payment was due and we had some other real needs. After prayer, the Lord lead me to demonstrate Bibles at a nearby Bible school. I knew the Lord was selling for me again as I wrote orders as fast as I could. In approximately one hour I made $137 in commissions.

Sometimes as I prayed for guidance the Lord would say, "Do not go out to sell today, but work all day in King's Teens." Other days He would tell me to sell. Many times I would pray thus, "Lord, today I am very busy in King's Teens work and I only have half an hour to spend in selling. Where shall I go?" Then I would go and obey the thought He put in my mind. Most of the time I would knock at a door, not knowing who the people were, demonstrate the Bible, make a sale, and be back home in half an hour. The very few times I failed I had gone out in my own strength, not taking time to pray and ask for His directions. During these Bible-selling days I was able to pray with many people and lead some to know the Lord. It was a blessed ministry, but I knew that someday the Lord would have me in King's Teens full time.

Finally came the day when I was so busy there wasn't time to sell Bibles. This was what the Lord was waiting for. He was gently forcing me to trust Him further in this life of living by faith. I put my demonstration Bible on the shelf, trusting God's promise that He would take care of all our needs. I Corinthians 9:14: "Even so hath the Lord ordained that they which preach the gospel should live of the gospel." This was a big step for us. We now had no visible means of support. The crutch of selling

Bibles was gone and with trembling hearts we were launching out farther from the shore and saying, "Lord, here we are."

We considered it a great privilege to live by faith, although it was not our choice but rather the Lord's. If we had not left our jobs and started to live by faith, we would have been disobedient to Him. I do not believe that just anyone can decide to live by faith and have the Lord supply his needs. I remember once a pastor friend of mine came to see me and said he had decided that he was going to tell his church that he did not want them to pay him a salary any more as he thought it would be a thrill to live by faith. I warned him, "Brother, be careful and be sure that this is what the Lord wants you to do. Living by faith is not your choice but rather God's. If God has chosen your church to pay your salary, you are going to find it pretty rugged trying to live by faith, out of the will of the Lord."

I wish that everyone could have the experience of living "by faith" for a period of time. We have found that the first requirement is a clean heart toward God and our fellow man. The Bible says in Psalm 66:18, "If I regard iniquity in my heart, the Lord will not hear me." My wife and I know that this verse is literally true. I discovered that I couldn't even have a good fight with my wife. Viv and I called Monday our business meeting day with the Lord. On this day we would present all our financial needs to Him. Most of us are prone to pray only for those things which we ourselves cannot solve. Right at the start the Lord began to teach us that nothing is too large or too small to bring to Him in prayer. We seek His guidance in shopping, buying groceries or clothing, and He guides us to the right store and in every appointment.

Before praying, Viv and I would claim Matthew 18:19: "Again I say unto you, that if two of you shall agree on earth as touching anything that they shall ask, it shall be done for them of my Father which is in heaven." We then would write down all of the needs coming up that week and present them audibly in prayer to the Lord. Our house payment of $50 was due on the fifteenth and near that time we would tell Him about that, also about other needs such as money for groceries, new shoes for Michael, $6.00 for gas and oil, etc. We would add up the total, plus our tithe, and present that amount to the Lord for the week. After requesting this money from Him, Viv and I would then thank the Lord for the money, even before we had received it, as we prayed according to His instructions and believed I John 5:14, 15: "And this is the confidence that we have in Him, that, if we ask anything according to His will, He heareth us: and if we know that He hears us, whatsoever we ask, we know that we have the petitions that we desired of Him."

Each week it was a thrilling experience to watch the Lord answer this prayer. We never knew whom He would use, but invariably if we expected money from some certain individual, He would not use that person. The Lord insisted that we look not at individuals for our needs, but to Him. Occasionally the Devil would trap Viv or me on something. As soon as this happened, it was like turning off water. Our needs were not supplied. Perhaps it could be that I became irritated at Vivian for something and even forgot about it. As we would see the food leaving our pantry shelf and no money or food coming in to replace it, invariably Viv and I would begin to seek the Lord to find out where the trouble was. As we prayed and tried to explain our need of food, the Lord would remind us that it was not His fault, but ours. We then would begin to search our hearts individually and ask Him to reveal the sin. Soon the Lord would reveal to me my irritation at my wife because she did not remember to tell me, until it was too late, that I had a phone call from a pastor asking me to speak, or even such little things as having her wake me up too late, or not ironing my shirts properly. One time we went out to speak at a conference and in the morning when I prepared myself for the day, I found Viv had not remembered to pack my Fast Teeth, a preparation to keep my false teeth in place. I could visualize my teeth jumping around in my mouth as I tried to speak. This time I really was irritated at her. The Lord then reminded me that my heart was in no condition to speak or help anyone until I apologized to my wife and got things right. This I did, and then God blessed.

A number of times on other occasions, even as we asked the Lord to forgive us and asked one another for forgiveness, while we were still on our knees, people knocked on our door with either money or food. We discovered that it was not hard to get in accord with one another when we would get hungry, for we knew that if we did not ask for forgiveness, we would not eat.

CHAPTER XI

Prayer Is Essential

I am convinced that no work of God can carry on without those who will help carry the load in prayer and that God does nothing except in answer to prayer. At the start of King's Teens, the Lord gave me two prayer partners, Kenny Johnson and Grover Cannon, and occasionally others would join us. For over three years we met each Monday night in the basement of The Beanery (a store owned by Grover Cannon opposite Franklin High School in Seattle). Our prayer meetings usually lasted most, or all, of the night. Here we bore the birth pangs for many souls who were born again in the King's Teens Club meetings. In these prayer meetings we would pray for just one need at a time, and we would continue to pray for that need until we had God's answer. We would pray down the barriers, and then later we would go out to possess the land or promises we had received from Him in prayer. I also met, whenever I could, with another group of men who came together every Tuesday night for prayer in downtown Seattle, under the direction of Axel Fredeen, a Seattle businessman. There was no nine o'clock closing time for this prayer meeting either. Men stayed together and prayed until the burden lifted, whether it was 11:00 P.M. or 2:00 A.M. With men praying together in one accord, things had to happen—and they did.

One of the great moments I will never forget was just before I started the King's Teens work. I went to the men's prayer meeting and told them how God had called me to combat juvenile delinquency through Christianity and asked them to pray for me that I might fulfill this task. Axel asked me to kneel at a chair, and then the men gathered around me and laid their hands on me and prayed that God would set me aside for this ministry. I believe that night God commissioned and anointed me for this task, and I have never been the same since.

Every week scores of teenagers were finding Christ as their personal Savior in King's Teens. I know that God used these prayer meetings to lay the foundation for my future work of founding King's Garden and its many affiliated works. Without these prayer warriors we could not have had the spiritual strength to carry on nor would we have seen King's Teens spread throughout the northwest.

At the beginning of our walk of faith, we wondered just how God wanted us to live. Then one day God sent Fred Renich to us to encourage us in our walk of faith and to instruct us. Fred was a Christian worker who had been living by faith for some time. My wife and I will never forget his remark to us: "If you expect hamburger every day, that is what you will get, but if you expect a beef roast with all the trimmings, He can just as easily supply that." This was a great lesson to us.

Vivian received a promise from the Lord that day that He would keep us on the same plane as we had lived when working for a salary, and she began to plan her meals as she had always done, but allowing God to plan the menu with her.

The Lord spoke to many different people, even some people we hardly knew, and at other times, some of our many friends, to supply our needs. For example, the Lord laid it on the hearts of the Fred Rady family to give us our Sunday meat, and for a time they came every Saturday with a roast. Then He would speak to Kenny Johnson or someone else to give us vegetables and other foods. When there was company coming—and we had much company in those days—invariably someone would bring a roast, a ham, or a chicken and other extra food. One day the Lord sent in a ham when we were entertaining the Grover Cannon family. Some time later the Cannons visited us again and ate with us. Again we had a ham. Grover remembered having had ham the last time they ate with us. Knowing how we lived, he remarked, "Evidently the Lord loves ham because He gives the Martins so much of it." Many times the Lord gave us treats of food that normally, if we were buying, we would have felt we could not afford. Other times only the bare essentials were provided, but we never lacked for something to eat.

"Living by faith" was quite exciting at times and very interesting. It required much prayer and, above all, complete obedience to the Lord. Some of our needs were so trifling that at times we hesitated to bring them to Him—praying for a nickel or dime to put into a parking meter, a place to park the car while downtown beside a parking meter that still had half an hour or more unexpired time, ten cents for a phone call, three cents for a postage stamp, gasoline enough to get home from a meeting. Many times I have started out in some direction to keep an appointment, with only enough gasoline in the car to go one way, trusting the Lord to get me back home again. I never walked home once, but all I can say is that sometimes the Lord must have made the gasoline stretch. Other times He would speak to someone to give me money. He never once failed me.

The privileges of living by faith are manifold. There are blessings in so many ways—some in disguise. Over and over again the Lord has demonstrated His ability to provide us with everything, including clothing. Most people have to purchase their needs from a store—a suit of clothes, a dress, or other articles. They need to choose the color, material, size, and style. For us, most of the time, it has not been necessary to give thought to what kind of a suit, dress, or shoes we should have. The Lord gives us just what we should have. He chooses the color and kind of suit and sends it to us.

Most people have to break in their shoes, but my shoes have already been broken in for me by someone else. God knows my size, and He even sends me socks and shirts. Following is a typical illustration: As I was in need of clothes, I prayed, "Lord, you know summertime is coming, and I would like a light colored suit. Would you provide me with one?"

A short time later I received a suit from a lady who said, "My husband passed away, and I would like you to have his summer suit." Sure enough, it was just the right size and the light color of God's choice.

When my daughter Joyce was to be married, I knew I would need a good, dark suit. As I looked over my clothes, I realized I did not have one suitable for the occasion, so we started to pray for one. We reminded the Lord it would be conspicuous for me to wear a light suit as I was to give my daughter away. A short time later I was invited to visit a man to see some things he had for us. As I came to see him, he said, "Mike, I have one of my suits I would like to give you, if you can wear it." Of course, it was a dark blue suit just the kind I needed, and again the right size. He also gave me some shoes he had, and I was arrayed in fine shape for the wedding—outfitted by the Lord.

Another time Viv and I needed clothes. It was at Easter, a time when most people like to have something new. We prayed together and told the Lord, "We would each like to have a new suit, one for Vivian and one for me." Just a few days later we received a check in the mail from my sisters and brothers in Bellingham, Washington. They had each put in some money, and they wrote us that they thought it was a wonderful thing for us to serve the Lord and they felt they would like to help us by sending enough money for a suit for each of us. Only God revealed our need to them as we had not told them we were praying for clothes. We praised and thanked God and my brothers and sisters for this gift.

Here is another example of how God provided. One day my brother, Vernon Martin, and his family came to visit us from Bellingham. This special day when they decided to come was one of those days when we were completely out of money. We had no food, except for a few staples, but we still had our confidence in the Lord. Viv and I met together in prayer before they came and told the Lord, "Vernon and his family are coming today. They do not know that we are trusting You for our food or what it means to live by faith and will You please, Lord, see that we have food for them?" After this prayer, we rechecked our assets, looking afresh in all of our pockets for money. We even looked under the cushions of the davenport and overstuffed chair to see if any money was there. When we had scraped all of our money together, we had only enough to buy a pound of coffee and a few potatoes. To Scandinavians, coffee is a must. We still did not have butter, milk, bread, meat, or dessert. We knew that we should have those things, but all we could do was start towards providing the meal, believing that the Lord would do the rest.

Many times the Lord used the mail to provide money for our needs, but when we began to look at the mailbox instead of to the Lord, He was displeased. This day we waited for the mailman to come. We were praying and hoping, but when he came, he had no mail for the Martins.

About three in the afternoon, Vernon, Doris, and their three children came, and we gave them coffee and visited for a while, talking about the family and other things. Frankly, I was becoming a little worried and so decided to take them out for a drive to allow the Lord more time to provide (as though He needed my help). After we left, Viv sat thinking and praying. After a while, she decided to take a bath and while in the bathtub, she continued praying for some money or groceries. The Lord then spoke to her and told her to look in her purse. She told the Lord she had already looked, but He reminded her of an old purse she had discarded some time ago. Viv ran downstairs and found the purse on the shelf and there, sure enough, she found just a small amount of change. When I came back, I immediately got Viv aside so that the others could not hear me and asked anxiously, "Viv, has the Lord provided yet?"

She replied, "A little, but still not enough. Keep praying." She handed me the money she had found in her old purse and asked me to go to the store for a quarter of a pound of butter, a loaf of bread, and a quart of milk. We still lacked meat and dessert. We did not say a thing to our company about the need, but continued to pray, believing that in some way the Lord would solve our problem.

I went to the store and got the things Viv had asked me to get, and she went ahead with the preparations for the meal as though she had all the ingredients necessary for a full-course meal. Shortly before dinner Vernon said, "Oh, I forgot something." He went out to the car and brought in a beef roast, already cooked, and a watermelon. We never did tell Vernon and Doris, but just praised the Lord silently. While I cut the watermelon, Viv put the roast in the oven to warm. How good to serve a God who looks after every detail!

Viv and I have never believed that, because we were serving the Lord, we should ever have to make apologies for our clothes, the food we served, or even our accommodations. We have discovered that God takes care of us according to that living standard which we pray for and expect to receive from Him. We have never had to apologize by saying, "You know we work for the Lord and these are the best clothes the Lord can give us." We have had times of testing, but that is true in any person's life, and it is true also for us who live by faith. We can say that we have proved that God's Word never fails.

Psalm 37:3, 4, 5: "Trust in the Lord, and do good; so shalt thou dwell in the land, and verily thou shalt be fed. Delight thyself also in the Lord; and He shall give thee the desires of thine heart. Commit thy way unto the Lord; trust also in Him; and He shall bring it to pass."

CHAPTER XII

The Prophet's Chamber

Viv and I had much company, and although we had three bedrooms, because of the size of our family, it was necessary to crowd in together when we had visitors overnight. One day we heard that Dr. and Mrs. N. A. Jepson had a "prophet's chamber" (a room reserved for visiting missionaries, ministers, and other full-time workers for the Lord). Vivian, realizing our need for more room to entertain God's servants, said that we too should pray for a prophet's chamber. This struck a responsive chord in my heart, and we began to pray together for this need. One day, shortly thereafter, while Viv was reading the Bible, she read this verse: "Let us make a little chamber, I pray thee, on the wall; and let us set for him there a bed, and a table, and a stool, and a candlestick: and it shall be, when he cometh to us, that he shall turn in thither" (II Kings 4:10). When she told me this, Viv and I came to the conclusion that God gave us this verse as a command and as His approval of our building a prophet's chamber.

Not long after this, a man we did not know, by the name of Tim, came to see us. He told us that our friend, Grover Cannon, had told him that we were praying for a man to build us a prophet's chamber and that God had told him that he was the man He wanted to build it for us. It was quite a thrill to us to have God speak to this man to answer our prayer. We knew that this was a real seal from the Lord that this was His will. We had no money, so it was a challenge and test to our faith, but we reasoned that if the Lord wanted us to have a prophet's chamber, surely He would take care of the cost. We had an upstairs back porch overlooking Puget Sound which was ideal for this purpose. We took Tim upstairs and showed him the porch we wanted enclosed. He said it would require considerable work but that it could be done. Then he turned to us and said, "Shall I order the lumber and materials COD?"

Viv and I looked at one another in agreement and said, "Yes, Tim, send the materials COD, and we will pay the bill when it comes."

Tim took the measurements and called the lumber company on the phone and ordered the materials. We had no idea how much money it would take, and we did not tell him that we did not have any money. But we knew that God understood all about it.

It was wonderful to see how God answered this prayer. The next day, Friday, we received $100 in the mail. Very seldom did we receive so much money. We first thanked God and then tithed the money and purchased a few needed groceries. On Saturday we had $86 left and therefore assumed that this would be the amount of the lumber bill. The lumber did not come until Monday. When it arrived, we instructed the delivery man where to pile the lumber, and while he was doing this,

Viv and I knelt in prayer, reminding the Lord that we had to have money enough to pay this bill. While we were praying, the mailman came and left a letter containing a $1.00 bill, followed shortly by the delivery man who presented us with the lumber bill which amounted to $86.65. If God had not sent that $1.00 just at that time we would not have had enough money. After tithing the $1.00, we still had enough money to buy a loaf of bread. How wonderful it is to have a God who takes care of the smallest details!

With the money we gave a tract to the delivery man, and after he left, we again knelt and praised the Lord for that which He had done. Surely the Lord's blessing and approval was in the building of this prophet's chamber!

Tim came the next day and started to build. He worked a few days, then he did not come for four days. When Tim came back after his absence, he told us the following story: "Three years ago I had a bad accident while working on the water front as a longshoreman. I was hit with a crane in the back so hard that my stomach burst open and my bowels gushed out in front. The blow also broke a number of vertebrae. As my back healed slowly, after months in the hospital, the cartilage in my back grew together in the wrong way. Quite often something happens to my back, and I have to bend over double, and it takes two or three days before I can straighten up again. Because of this, I have not been able to work for over three years except occasionally to help someone as I am helping you." We could see that this injury was a great trial to Tim, but he told us not to worry, that if we were not in too big a hurry he would be able to complete the prophet's chamber for us.

One day I told Tim how the Lord had recently healed Vivian in answer to prayer. My wife had not been feeling well for some time and when she went for a checkup at the doctor's, he discovered that she had a tumor. This tumor, the doctor explained, was serious and must be removed immediately as it might even be malignant. We told the doctor that we were home missionaries living by faith and could not do anything without first praying and asking God for His directions. It was difficult to explain our belief to the doctor, but we endeavored to do so by saying, "We believe God uses doctors to help people in their sickness and operations, but we also believe that God is not limited to doctors, that He is still the Great Physician and can heal any and all diseases, including tumors. All we can do, doctor, is pray and ask Him if He wants you to operate or if He wants us to trust Him for the healing." The doctor again tried to impress us with the urgency of a quick decision as we left his office.

We prayed for some days, and then one Sunday evening as we were getting ready for church, the Lord spoke to my wife and said, "Go to Mr. Killgore." The Lord had used this Christian and Missionary Alliance minister many times in praying for the sick. Instead of going to church, we went over to see this minister. He instructed us out of the Word in regard to healing, bringing many scriptures to our attention: Isaiah 53:5, "But he was wounded for our transgressions, he was bruised for our iniquities: the chastisement of our peace was upon him; and with his stripes we are healed." Matthew 8:16, 17, "When the even was come, they brought unto him many that were possessed with devils: and he cast out the spirits with his word, and healed all that were sick: That it might be fulfilled which was spoken by Esaias the prophet, saying, himself took our infirmities, and bare our sicknesses." James 5:14-16, "Is any sick among you? Let him call for the elders of the church; and let them pray over him, anointing him with oil in the name of the Lord: And the prayer of faith shall save the sick, and the Lord shall raise him up; and if he have committed sins, they shall be forgiven him. Confess your faults one to another, and pray one for another, that ye may be healed. The effectual fervent prayer of a righteous man availeth much."

As we listened to these verses, our faith was increased, and we both believed that God was going to heal her. Mr. Killgore then anointed my wife with oil, according to James 5:14-16, and prayed for her. Viv expected that her body would be touched immediately and that she would feel better instantly, but instead she felt worse and her faith began to waver. The Lord, however, gave Ednalee Lewis, one of our King's Teens workers, and me faith to believe that God had touched Viv's body. Viv would say, "I don't think I am healed because if I was, I would feel better." Daily, though, the Lord gave Ednalee and me the assurance that Viv was healed. Together we continued to thank the Lord for healing Viv even as she continued to feel worse. This went on for about 30 days, and then one evening she passed the tumor. We decided that the healing should be verified by a doctor, and we went to a specialist for women, for a complete physical checkup. The doctor said he could see the scar where the tumor had been but that there was nothing wrong now. God had done a perfect job.

As we told Tim this, he asked, "Do you think the Lord could heal me now?" I told Tim that the Lord was no respecter of persons and that He would heal but that He expected us to believe and trust Him.

A short time after this, Tim attempted to get a settlement for this accident from the state. The state refused to settle but rather decided that there should be another operation on his back to insert a steel brace in his back. This would keep him from doubling over although he would never be able to bend again. He would never be able to be gainfully employed again but at least the brace would prevent him from bending double. Tim came to us again to ask about healing and I told him he had to make up his mind what to do. "Tim, either believe the Lord, that He is going to heal your body, or trust in the doctors, but you cannot ask the Lord to heal you with the thought in mind that if He doesn't heal, you can always have the operation. You must believe that He is going to heal your body."

Tim prayed over the weekend, and on Monday morning he came and said, "I have called and canceled the operation. Will you go with me to be anointed and prayed for?" Again we went over to Mr. Killgore of Simpson Bible School. He explained to Tim about healing, and then Tim was anointed with oil. While we were on our knees, Tim jumped to his feet and cried, "I've been healed. I've been healed." I, too, knew he had been healed because I had felt the touch of the Lord on my own body as he was prayed for. The next day he went back to the longshoreman's job where he had been working and reported to them that he had been healed. Tim was checked over completely by the doctors and even though they could not explain it, they pronounced him cured. Tim got his old job back and immediately was able to carry heavy weights on his back again. As far as I know, he is well to this day.

I believe in divine healing but I do not believe that the Lord is confined to this method. I know the Lord has provided doctors to minister to our bodies. Luke was a physician. The Lord must be the one to get all the glory whatever method is used. As we lived by faith, we found that He was not only sufficient for the money we needed, but He was able to provide our spiritual and physical needs as well.

CHAPTER XIII

God Provides My Transportation

Providing transportation for teenagers is hard on cars, but over and over again the Lord demonstrated to us that we were in the center of His will by even providing cars for us. We purchased the first car while I was at Simpson Bible Institute. One of the men who was graduating from the school had an old jalopy which he wanted to sell. It was in pretty good shape, considering its age. When I inquired how much he wanted for it, he told me he would sell me the car for $75. This was a bargain and I told him I would buy it. I then gave him the $25 we had saved and started driving the car daily, going back and forth to work. Just before the second payment was due, the man we bought the car from came to us and said, "The Lord has heard your prayers. A man came and paid the balance of the car in full for you. You do not owe me anything." He then gave me the bill of sale. Some time later when I went to pay my tuition at Simpson, I discovered that someone, possibly the same person, had paid my tuition also in full for a year. I do not know for sure who paid the money for these things, but I do know it was God who caused him to do this for us. I now had a car, my tuition was paid, and God was blessing in a remarkable way as I was spending more and more time in working with teenagers.

Every Tuesday evening we used the car for transportation for our King's Teens meetings. That car seemed to stretch out as I packed in the kids. I would drive around the Ballard area in Seattle, picking up young people, and often we would have 10, 12, 14 and sometimes as many as 16 in that 5 passenger car. As I drove the teenagers to and from the meeting they would sing choruses, and it almost seemed that the car chugged and knocked in an effort to keep time with the music. It was quite a car, but one day it just folded up, much like the "one hoss shay."

For about four months we were without a car, which made it very difficult for us, walking to church, taking the bus to work, and so forth. I was unable to pick up the young people for King's Teens, and some of them were unable to come because of this. Viv and I daily brought the matter to the Lord, endeavoring to explain to Him our need for a car. We even began to question why, doubting God. One day we touched the hem of His garment in prayer (Matthew 9:20). We knew we had prayed through and had a real witness in our hearts that God was going to supply us with a car, and we began to thank Him for the car He was going to send us. We knew the Lord was either going to give us a car or send the money for one. One morning, shortly after this, we received a check for $1,500 in the mail. This was the first time that we had received such a large sum of money. It was from a man we hardly knew. In fact, I had only seen him once or twice in my life, and would not have known him well enough to call him by name if I had met him on the street. In the letter was a slip of paper telling us that the Lord had told him to send us this money, and then he concluded the short note with these startling words: "It is not going to be long until the Lord comes, and I do not want to be caught with much money in the bank."

We knew definitely this money was for the car, but evidently not for a new one because we could not buy a new car with this amount of money. As was our custom, we first paid our tithe of $150, leaving us $1,350. We received this gift during World War II, when there were only a few new cars being manufactured. The new ones which were available were on a high priority, and therefore we felt we should look for a good used car.

During the time we were without a car, usually we would take a short cut through Woodland Park on our way to church on Sunday and on prayer meeting night. As we would walk through the zoo, we would enjoy the privilege of seeing the various wild animals and birds. Then one Sunday morning, shortly after receiving this money, we decided to walk along the street to our church instead of through the park. About three blocks away from the church we saw a Ford, with a big sign on it, "For Sale." This car was just one year old and appeared to be in tiptop shape. As Viv saw the sign, she said, "There's our car." I was not sure, as I was still wishing and praying for a new car, but she had the witness immediately that this was the car we were to purchase. All during the church service, I am sorry to say, our thoughts were on the car we had seen. On the way home, we stopped and looked at it again and asked the owner how much he was asking for the car. Mr. Fisher told us he would sell it for $1,800, which was a good buy. We told him we had been praying for a car so that we could use it in our King's Teens work and tried to explain to him that we were living by faith, which we found difficult to explain. We told him we believed this might be the car the Lord had for us, but we were not sure. We finally went on our way, telling him we would call him after we had had time to pray about the matter.

As we prayed, we asked the Lord, if this was His car for us, "Please have the owner reduce the price of the car; then we will know this is the car." Even while we were praying, the man called and told us that in view of the kind of work we were doing he would reduce the price $100. Immediately we told him over the phone that we would buy the car and that I would go up and give him $1,350 as a down-payment towards it.

My family met together and thanked the Lord and then Curtis and I went up to the owner and gave him the money. He turned the key over to us, but we told him we would not take the car until we had it completely paid for. We told him that the Lord who had supplied this first amount would supply the balance of $350. God gave us faith to tell Mr. Fisher, "To demonstrate to you that this is of the Lord, 30 days from now we will be back and give you the other $350. I do not work at any job and have no income, but my family and I trust the Lord and know He will supply this need." This was not said presumptuously, but rather it was what the Lord had told us. Mr. Fisher was impressed, but still a little dubious. He did not, of course, understand about this faith in God that we were talking about. Mr. Fisher agreed to keep the car in his garage for us until we got the money. We went home and rejoiced in what the Lord had done and was going to do.

We hoped and prayed that the money might come in just one sum, but it did not, and just a very little money over our expenses came in from day to day. At the end of 30 days we still lacked $180 to pay for the car in full. We couldn't understand why the money had not come. Usually when we had special needs like this, Viv and I would spend more time in prayer. We agreed to make the following Monday a day of fasting (abstaining from food) and prayer, asking the Lord for the money to take care of this need. As we prayed, we reminded Him of His promise to supply this need and how Mr. Fisher was expecting us to come with the money because we had told him our God was going to supply.

While we were still on our knees God began to speak to my heart—that I was still longing for a new car and I needed to accept the car God was sending without any reservation. I had even gone as far as telling Joe Brill that I would possibly sell him this car when we had secured it. It was necessary for me to arise from my knees and write a card to Joe saying I could not sell him this car as this was God's choice for us. After the card was written, I again fell on my knees and thanked the Lord for this used car he was going to give us. Immediately we heard the doorbell ring, and when we opened the door, a man stood there with a check in his hand. He said, "The Lord told me I was to give you this a few days ago but I neglected to do it." The check was for $200, just the amount we needed—$20 for our tithe and $180 for the car. We praised the Lord together as we told him about our praying for just this sum in order to get the car God had directed us to buy. He rejoiced with us and said he should have obeyed the Lord when he was told to bring the money earlier. However, I told him this was God's timing as I had to get something right before God could supply this money.

When we went up to get the car, we told Mr. Fisher how God had performed this another miracle for us. We then asked him if he would allow us to pray for him and his family. He granted us permission, and we all stood with bowed heads as I prayed and thanked God for hearing and honoring our prayers. We know that this was a real testimony for Mr. Fisher and his family as they saw how the Lord takes care of His own children. This car was a real blessing to us and never gave us any difficulty.

CHAPTER XIV

Our Work Is Blessed

From the very day that I said yes to the Lord and started King's Teens, God's hand of blessing has been upon it. We have had various other types of meetings along with the club meetings, such as rallies and King's Teens banquets. The very first year of King's Teens, many teenagers found Christ as their personal Savior.

One day a number of the King's Teens members came to me and told me that they had either an unsaved father or mother, or both, and they were concerned. We began to pray together and think of how their parents could be reached for the Lord. We finally decided to have a St. Valentine's banquet and invite all the parents to come. Daily we prayed for these parents to be saved. We began to gather food for the banquet and planned an interesting program.

It was marvelous to see how in answer to prayer the Lord sent most of the parents to this first St. Valentine's banquet. After a good chicken fricassee dinner and a musical program, I stood on a chair so that all could see me and began to speak. We could feel the Spirit of the Lord present. While I was preaching, one of the mothers came up and began to tug at my coat. I was embarrassed and frustrated and tried to ignore her and go on with my sermon, but I found this was impossible. Finally I stopped and leaned over to ask her, "What do you want?"

She said, "I want to get saved."

This was a new situation to me as I had never encountered anything of this kind before. I thought it was only possible for a person to be saved at the conclusion of the message so I told her, "You can't get saved yet, as I am not through speaking." Nevertheless, she was so insistent (and I am thankful she was), that I asked one of our counselors to take this mother into another room to pray with her. Later she came back and gave a glowing testimony telling us that she had found Christ as her Savior. Since this thrilling experience, I will now stop while I am speaking anyplace, to help a person to find Christ. That night God spoke to a number of the parents, and the first annual St. Valentine's banquet was a real success.

Every year the Lord has blessed each King's Teens annual banquet in a remarkable way. We have had many wonderful speakers, including Bob Pierce, Joe Brill, Willis Shank, Jimmy Stewart, Torrey Johnson, and many others. Hilding Halvarson, well-known Seattle singer, has been our song leader each year. I especially remember two of these banquets. Willis Shank was the speaker at one of them. There were approximately 500 present. As is the custom, at the conclusion of the message Willis gave an opportunity for those unsaved to accept Christ. The Holy Spirit was moving in the hearts of the teenagers, and they started coming forward, weeping, to get saved. It was a sight which would bring rejoicing to the heart of every saint. We then asked those who were Christians if they would like to yield their lives to the Lord for service and, if so, to write their names on the white paper hearts hidden in the programs and to come forward to deposit them in a box at the head table. Willis, Hilding and I began to weep for joy as we saw scores of young people move to the front, weeping as they came. Everyone was touched by what took place at this glorious banquet.

At another St. Valentine's banquet, with approximately 750 teenagers present, Joe Brill was our speaker. At the conclusion of his message, he gave the invitation to all those who were not saved to give their hearts to the Lord. At first there was no response. Then all at once the young people near the platform went to their knees and began to pray, followed by row after row of others. There was a ripple like the waves of the sea as young people fell to their knees until almost every person was on his knees praying. I then asked if any who were praying wanted to be saved and needed someone to help pray for them. Hands were raised everywhere. That night again, many teenagers found Christ as their personal Savior.

We are thankful the Lord has saved many adults also through the work of King's Teens, both at our rallies and at the banquets. We have held many rallies at the Moore Theatre and other places in downtown Seattle and have seen the Spirit of God speak to many people, saving some and calling others into Christian service. At one rally, a Jewess was sitting in our audience, and after she listened to the message, she came forward and accepted Christ as her personal Savior. She also dedicated her life for Christian service at the same time and is now serving as a missionary in Europe.

God was blessing not only in the banquets and rallies, but also in the King's Teens Club meetings everywhere. At our Bainbridge Island club, the counselor began to hold weekly prayer meetings before the meetings and the teenagers agreed together that they would especially invite the unsaved boys and girls to come. They began to pray for 100% meetings, which meant that they were praying that every boy and girl who came would be saved before leaving the meeting. For a period of time every unsaved teenager who came to the meetings was saved. One boy who came to a King's Teens picnic had never heard of Christ before. That first night around the fireside he gave his heart to Christ. He became so thrilled with joy that he brought his mother and his sister to another King's Teens meeting and they, too, found Christ. Soon his whole family, except the father, made a profession of the Lord.

There were many outstanding conversions, and there was a great deal of joy in reaching the lost for Christ. One of these conversions was at the King's Teens Club in Maple Valley. A teenage girl was saved. She came from a home where Christ was unknown. She went home full of joy and told her mother she had found Christ. Her mother reprimanded her and said she did not want any such nonsense, that she did not want her girl to be a religious fanatic. The daughter did not say anything, but went into her bedroom. Before she went to bed, she prayed audibly and asked the Lord to save her mother and dad, who was working on a boat in Alaska. As her mother heard her daughter praying for her, she became angry and told her not to pray for her or her father. But every night her mother eavesdropped, and she heard her daughter praying for her.

Finally the mother wrote to her husband and told him she hoped he would come home soon because their daughter had become a religious fanatic and every night was kneeling and praying for God to save her mother and dad. The dad had had Christian influence as a boy. Instead of the letter having the desired effect, it put the father under conviction. When he returned home his wife expected him to chasten their daughter, but instead he said, "Honey, after I got that letter from you, I too gave my heart to the Lord, and I want you also to find Him." How wonderful it was to see that family make a stand for God! They really grew in the Lord. The first thing they did was to testify to the grocery clerk and she, too, found the Lord. At one of the King's Teens meetings the whole group came and told of what Christ had done for them all as a result of the daughter finding the Lord at a King's Teens meeting.

We have seen a touch of revival in some of the club meetings. At one such meeting Joe Brill was the speaker. He was unable to bring the message, for after he had read two Scripture verses, a teenage boy stood up and started to cry. He said, "I have sinned, and I want to get right with the Lord." His confession and cry for spiritual help put others under conviction and most of the young people began to cry and ask God for forgiveness.

Young people who were not saved began to cry out for salvation, and the entire meeting became a real revival. Our own church felt the impact of this touch of revival, and so did the parents and other young people.

Another interesting night was at a social of the King's Teens Club. Eddie Nolander of the Bible Crusaders was speaking, and when he gave the invitation no one responded. Then he said, "I sense the Devil is here to hinder you from making the right decision, but I rebuke you, Devil, in Jesus' Name!" Then he said, "Now, how many would really like to find the Lord?" I was standing at the back of the room, and as the young people sat with their heads bowed, the Lord spoke to me to ask some to accept Christ. So I touched a teenager on the shoulder, intending to speak to him. Before I could speak to him, down on his knees he went. So I began to touch this one and that one on the shoulder and it seemed that whoever I touched just dropped to his or her knees. I never even said a word. It was a meeting where the Lord took over and the teenagers were under deep conviction. The unsaved wanted to be saved. Eddie said, "All of you teenagers who want to find Christ, please go into this room," pointing to a kitchen off the social room where we were meeting. The kitchen was quickly filled, and then many more young people went out into the hall, where we were able to pray with them and lead them to Christ.

Every week similar things happened to make us so conscious that the time to reach people for Christ is when they are young. It seems that if boys or girls are going to get into trouble, they usually do so during the teenage years, but this also is one of the ages when it is the easiest for them to come to Christ.

The Lord has used King's Teens Clubs to call many young people into full-time service. I was at a ministers' conference, and two men came to me. One said, "Mike, do you remember me?"

Before me I saw a young, good looking minister, but I could not remember him at all. He said, "I got saved in your King's Teens Clubs. My name is————. Don't you remember me?"

Immediately after this the other minister came to me and said, "How are you, Mike? Do you remember me? God called me into His service at a King's Teen Club." The last time I had seen these two young men was when they were teenage members of King's Teens. They had changed considerably, making it impossible for me to remember them, but I did recognize their names when they told me who they were.

Many former King's Teens members are now ministers or ministers' wives, missionaries, and Christian workers throughout the world. I remember how God dealt with my own daughter Joyce, now Mrs. Rodney Brown, who is now a missionary in New Guinea. God asked her, at a regular King's Teens meeting, if she would be willing to dedicate her life to Him. Joyce stood to her feet in a meeting to tell how God had just called her to be a missionary for Him. As she spoke she wept, until finally she had to sit down. Afterwards she came to me and said, "Dad, I failed the Lord. I so wanted to tell the kids about Christ and how He had called me, but all I could do was cry." Joyce did not know until after the service that one of the girls we prayed with that night was Shirley Ann Holton, who said, "When I heard Joyce's testimony and saw her weep, I thought if Jesus can mean that much to a girl, I too want this Christ, and while Joyce was speaking, I gave my heart to Christ." What a joy it was to tell Joyce that her testimony had won a soul for Christ!

At every King's Teens meeting we had been giving an invitation to young people to make decisions for Christ. One day a man came to me and said, "Mike, you are making a big mistake by giving an invitation at every meeting. You should only do it once in a while." This man was a very fine Christian gentleman and much older in the Lord than I. So I reasoned he must be right. The next meeting I brought a message and closed with prayer without giving an invitation to accept Christ.

The following week at the time when we give people time for testimonies, a young man got to his feet and said, "Last week when you gave the message, at the close of the meeting I wanted to get saved but you did not give me a chance. This week if you give an invitation I am going to get saved." That young man did not have to wait for the end of the meeting, because right there we stopped and led him to Christ. Since that time at every King's Teens meeting we have given an invitation. How do I know what night someone may be waiting to find Christ? What would have happened if that young man had never come to King's Teens again or if he had died before he had a chance to be saved? God help me to be directed by the Holy Spirit and not by man.

CHAPTER XV

Maple Valley

King's Teens Clubs have been operating during the school year only, from September until June, when school closes. This normally left our summers quite free except for our King's Teens summer camp. I usually had approximately two and a half months open for other things.

One summer I was invited to be the interim pastor for the Community Church at Maple Valley, Washington. I was fairly well known in that area as we had a King's Teens Club there. God had blessed the King's Teens work in Maple Valley in an unusual way, and as I started to work in the Community Church, we saw God begin to work there also. When I began, there were only a few in Sunday school, and the church was not yet organized. During the summer we were able, with the Lord's help, to organize the church, call a pastor, and see the church and Sunday school more than double in number.

I started the work by going from house to house, visiting and talking with every person individually about the Lord. As I went into some of the homes, I met a number of people who had never before been exposed to the Gospel. I remember one old Icelandic lady I visited. When I asked her if she had a Bible, she looked at me questioningly. I endeavored to explain to her it was God's Word I wanted, "The Bible."

"When I came from Iceland," she said, "I took a Book with me. Maybe that's it." She told me she was not able to read the American language, but when she went to the trunk and took out her old Bible, I noticed it was written in the Icelandic language. Being a Scandinavian, I found I could understand certain words. I turned to John 3:16 and asked her to read it. She said she had not read Icelandic for so long that she did not know if she could read it or not, but she would try. She read something like this, "For God loves somebody—who was it? Who was God?" My heart went to her as I saw a lady here in the United States not knowing God just like someone in darkest Africa, where Christ is unknown.

I had a fertile mission field right in Maple Valley, and God helped me to win a number of souls for Christ during the summer. I remember one Sunday service especially. When I gave the invitation to those who were unsaved to accept Christ as their personal Savior, a number of people responded. Among them was one complete family, a husband, his wife and their two little children. As I talked to them, the husband said, "I want to be a Christian but I don't think I can. I have a number of bad habits." I explained to him that the Lord could forgive him and take away all his bad habits. "Even smoking?" he asked. I quoted to him Jeremiah 32:27: "Behold I am the Lord, the God of all flesh: is there any thing too hard for me?" I then explained to him how the Lord promised to forgive us our sins when we were sincere in asking pardon. "If we confess our sins, he is faithful and just to forgive us our sins, and to cleanse us from all unrighteousness" (I John 1:9). Then I went on to explain that salvation was not obtained by works of righteousness but by believing and accepting what the Bible said. If he would ask for forgiveness and then call on the Lord, asking Him to save him, He would do it. "For whosoever shall call upon the name of the Lord shall be saved" (Romans 10:13). As I gave him these wonderful promises, he said, "That is what I need." What a joy it was to have him and his wife and family kneel and pray. It was an instant transaction. God not only saved him and his family but delivered him completely from his cigarette habit as well.

It was during this time that I believe the Devil tried to kill me, seeing that God was using me to reach souls for the Lord. That summer we had an epidemic of accidents. We had two traffic accidents, one right after the other, which caused our insurance company to cancel my automobile insurance policy. I consider myself a fairly good driver. As a former owner of a service station and parking lot, I had driven every make of car. I had become an expert in parking cars. Then after I sold my service station, I drove tens of thousands of miles for the Richfield Oil Company, all without any accident. But now it seemed every time we went any place in the car, we were conscious that the Devil was trying to cause us to have another accident.

One day, when out on church visitation at Maple Valley, I turned into a driveway to call at a home when a car coming behind me hit my car broadside. Just before we collided, I had an opportunity to turn my car just enough so that it was not completely turned over. Although the cars were wrecked quite badly, I thought it a miracle that I was not injured. I could have been killed so easily. Because I had failed to signal that I was turning, it was my fault. We had no money and no insurance. I acknowledged my responsibility and told the other driver that though we had no money or insurance, we served the Lord and knew that He would take care of this need. The man threatened suit against us anyway, and his attorney contacted us immediately and gave us only 30 days to get the money together to take care of his client's car, or he would bring us to court. That night at the church prayer meeting service, I told the people how I had almost been killed that day. We praised the Lord together for His protection on my life. After the service that night, Mr. Joe Busch came up and pressed $40 into my hand and said that God asked him to help us pay for the accident. This was just a forerunner of many smaller gifts that came in from day to day until on the thirtieth day the Lord gave us just enough money not only to pay the attorney and the other man's car repairs, but ours also.

My wife and I became almost afraid of taking the car out. We just felt like the Devil was after us with all his might. Shortly after this accident, in driving through Seattle on a rainy Sunday, with Paul and Florence Turnidge, very good friends of ours who were also working with us in King's Teens, I put on my brakes to stop at a stop light, and the brakes failed. I hit the car ahead, but this time the collision was not quite as serious. When we brought the man's car to the garage and got the estimate, the man offered to settle his claim for $50 if we would pay it right there. We had the $50 which the Lord had given us just the day before for our house payment which was due on Monday, so we gave the man the money.

The next day Viv and I knelt before our davenport and prayed, explaining to Him how we had to take the $50 house payment and give it to settle for the accident. While we were still on our knees, Paul and Florence came over with $50, saying that the Lord had spoken to them even while they were praying, asking them to give us this money for our house payment. Truly the Lord was faithful to us, His servants.

With two accidents already, and fearful of more, all we could think to do was pray, so we began to pray that the Lord would protect us by His blood which He shed on Calvary. We prayed, "Lord, we plead the blood of Jesus over the car and over us as we drive down the street." Praise God, the accidents stopped! We believe the blood of Jesus is one weapon that Satan cannot get through. Now we use this protection wherever we go.

One day as Viv and I were praying together, I turned to her and said, "I feel that the Devil is going to try to make us have another accident today. Let us pray and ask for God's protection and cover the car and ourselves with the blood of Jesus." We prayed this prayer together and then went over to Sears and Roebuck to shop. Just as we drove out of the parking lot a car came swiftly towards us. We slammed on our brakes and made an abrupt stop. The cars were just touching each other when we got out, but there wasn't a dent or mark on either car. Praise God! We felt God showed us the accident that we would have had if we had not prayed and pleaded the blood of Christ for His protection.

While we were working in Maple Valley, one day when our own boy, Michael, was playing up in a tree, he fell about twenty feet, landing on the steel edge of a trunk. He split his forehead completely open. We were called by the friends who discovered him. When we arrived there, he was bleeding and practically unconscious, and we thought he was dead. We hurried and carried Michael to the car and drove swiftly to the hospital in Renton. On the way the Lord began to speak to Viv and me saying, "Is Michael still on the altar? Is he mine? If I take him to heaven, is it OK?" As we looked at our boy, bleeding, we were able to say, "He is Yours. You do with him as You will, and we will continue to serve You." God heard as we re-offered our son up to Him in sacrifice. He answered our prayers, and Michael fully recovered. The doctor said another half an inch and he would have lost his eye or would possibly have been killed. God is still our protector, although He does allow us to be tested to see if that which we put on the altar as a sacrifice is still there.

CHAPTER XVI

My Miracle Healing

The Lord was blessing our King's Teens work. We were working night and day, and many people were asking us to start a club in their area. I was traveling a good deal, visiting these places, going a little faster than was good for me physically.

I came back home from one trip before Christmas and took my family up to Bellingham to spend Christmas with my folks. I did not feel good on Christmas Day. I did not know just what was wrong, but I assumed that I was tired from overwork. My family told me they thought I was putting on weight, so when I returned to Seattle, I decided I should reduce. I began to take exercises of various kinds, and the more I exercised the worse I felt.

A few days after we had returned to Seattle, one of our King's Teens counselors, Allen Wood, came over to see me concerning his club. After discussing his problem, I told Allen how I felt physically, and we decided that perhaps I should go and see a doctor. I phoned my doctor and he told me to come down to see him immediately. As my wife was downtown, Allen drove me over to the doctor's office. I told the doctor I had a speaking engagement for that evening, but after his examination of me, he said, "You do not have a speaking engagement for tonight or for a few nights to come. You are going to the hospital."

It was a tremendous shock to be told that I had to go to the hospital. He said there was not even time to return home, but that I must enter the hospital immediately. Allen had waited for me, so he drove me to the hospital. The hospital called my wife and told her where I was. This news was a great shock to her also.

At the hospital they discovered I had a very bad heart condition. What I thought was fat was liquid in my system and my ankles were swelled and my whole body was bloated with fluid. For eight days I hovered between life and death. Finally, when I got a little better, I was moved to my home, and there I spent a few weeks in bed.

While I was still sick in bed, I began to pray, asking the Lord why it was that I was put in bed when we were so busy. It seemed for a period of time the Lord just let me rest and never spoke to me. I then prayed, "Please, Lord, help me to know the lesson you are trying to teach me in this sickness so that I won't have to go through this again." As I lay in bed the Lord became more precious to me as He began to reveal to me valuable lessons which He had not been able to reveal before because I was going too fast.

Both my wife and daughter were working full-time in King's Teens, endeavoring to keep up the work. One day I noticed Joyce's ankles were swollen and when I inquired why, I discovered she had been standing at the mimeograph machine for a number of days endeavoring to print all the materials needed for our expanding King's Teens work. I began to complain to the Lord in prayer, explaining to Him that it was not right that Joyce had to stand on her feet for such long periods of time, running the mimeograph machine, until her feet swelled. I told Him we needed additional help or a printing press so that we could do the printing work ourselves more efficiently.

Then the Lord began to speak to me inaudibly, saying, "Why don't you ask me for a printing press?" These words startled me. I actually had not thought of really asking for a printing press. Therefore, since He asked me to do so, I prayed just once this short prayer, "Lord, please give me a printing press." I knew immediately God had heard me and that my prayer was answered. "And this is the confidence that we have in him, that, if we ask any thing according to his will, he heareth us: And if we know that he hears us, whatsoever we ask, we know that we have the petitions that we desired of him" (I John 5:14, 15).

I called my wife and said, "Viv, the Lord has just given us a printing press." Startled, she looked at me and then looked around the room as though looking for a printing press, but wondering what I was speaking about. I explained how the Lord had told me to ask Him for a printing press, and that He had given me a witness that my prayer was heard and answered. I was very ill at the time, and Viv did not know if I was rational or not. I told her she would have to get Curtis, our 16 year old boy, to change his high school course and take printing so that he could operate the press when the Lord had given it to us.

As I insisted on this, to pacify and humor me because of my illness, she contacted the principal of the Ballard High School and told him, "My husband is sick, almost dying and he is insisting that our boy, Curtis, change his course so that he can take printing. Could you please do this for us?" The principal was gracious and understanding, and even though the new semester had started, he granted my request and gave Curtis the opportunity of taking printing in high school. In the next chapter I will tell the miracle story of how God gave us the press.

When I was a little stronger, the doctor asked that I be brought to his office for another examination. I thought I was getting better but after his examination, he found I had developed a tumor on my kidneys. My blood pressure was 256, and I was still in a very weakened condition. Although my heart was very bad, the doctor said he would have to try to get me strong enough so that he could operate on me. It was very depressing to me and to my family to contemplate an operation on top of all this sickness. Viv and I returned home very disheartened and wondered, "Why, God, why all this, when there is so much work to be done in King's Teens?"

As we entered our home, we did not know that the Lord had prepared a group of four men to come and pray for me that I might be healed. These men were waiting for us in our front room: the Rev. Fred Renich, the Rev. Melvin Dahlstrom, the Rev. Hegge Iverson, and Axel Fredeen. They told Viv and me they had come because God had instructed them to come and pray for me that I might be healed. I knew that the Lord could heal, but I had never experienced it in my own body. All I could think of when I came home and saw those men was, "Don't they realize how sick I am? Why bother me at this time?" Viv felt the same way because she could see I was very weary and ill from my trip to the doctor's office. As I tried to relax, Rev. Iverson began to tell me how he once was on the verge of death through tuberculosis and that for over a year he hovered between life and death, and one day God revealed to him that he could be healed through His Word in James 5:13-15.

Mr. Hegge said that as he claimed these promises from the Bible, the Lord honored it and he was completely cured. He also told of his sister who had tuberculosis of the bone and of how her foot had shriveled so that she was unable to walk. She, too, was anointed with oil, and the Lord healed her and even restored the anklebone so that she now walks normally. As he told me of these things, and the other men also told of their experiences of how the Lord had healed them, I began to have hope. I had known of God's promises and had seen my wife healed, but it seems that it is much easier to have faith for others to be healed than for yourself when you are ill. But as faith came into my heart, I asked the men to anoint me with oil and pray for me that I might be healed. As they laid hands on me, anointing me with oil and praying, God touched my body. I felt the Spirit of God touch me, and I knew in my own heart, even though I still felt sick, that I was healed. We rejoiced together and praised and thanked God for healing me.

My strength was not restored immediately, but I knew I was healed. I still looked sick, but I told everyone how the Lord had touched my body. I had another appointment with the doctor on Tuesday as he wanted to check further so that he could see how soon he could operate on me. I told him that God had touched my body and healed me miraculously. He looked at me very dubiously, but he took my blood pressure and it had dropped over 50 points. From there I was taken to the X-ray room and X-rayed again, but now they could not find any tumor on my kidney. God had removed it. Truly the Lord had performed a tremendous miracle for me. The doctor could not explain it, but he had to admit that something had happened to me. Even though he did not acknowledge it, I knew and told him again that God had healed me.

The King's Teens banquet was to be held on Friday of this same week. I knew that I was healed and therefore I felt I should plan on attending this banquet. As I told my doctor and nurse of my plans, they both endeavored to discourage me from attending. They felt I was presumptuous and foolish, for they did not really believe that I was healed, although they could not explain the great improvement in my health.

The conviction grew on me that if I was truly healed, I should testify to the King's Teens kids how God had healed me and, I reasoned, where could I better do this than at the banquet? My wife was in accord with me, for she also believed I was healed and, therefore, even though I was very weak, I attended this banquet. My nurse was present in the audience, watching carefully, I am sure, to help me in case something happened to me. People, looking at me, could see my pallor and that undoubtedly I was very ill. As I stood at the rostrum and told people how God had touched my body, I was so weak I had to brace myself in order to keep standing. I gave my testimony and told of the miracle God wrought in my body by healing me. Even as I gave this testimony, God began to strengthen my body and from that moment on, I continued to gain strength. I believe if I had not taken this first step of faith and told others of my healing, the Lord would have been grieved and my healing would not have been completed.

CHAPTER XVII

Testings and Trials

As I began to get stronger, I was reminded again of the promise I had received while ill in bed, of a printing press. One day I heard of a printing shop for sale so I made an appointment to see it. I took Viv and Curtis with me that afternoon to look at this equipment. As we talked with the man we discovered he was a Christian. We told him of our need for printing presses and how we had been praying for equipment and that the Lord had promised us a printing press. After we inspected his printing equipment, it seemed to us it was just what we needed. As we stood beside the presses, we asked the man to join us in prayer to ask the Lord if this was the equipment He wanted us to purchase. As we prayed, the Holy Spirit witnessed to each one of us that this was the printing equipment the Lord had reserved for us. The man quoted a ridiculously low price of $500 for the two presses, paper cutter, fonts of type, and other things necessary for a small, fairly complete printing shop.

Sometimes when God has given me a promise, the Devil tries to interfere, little doubts enter in, and I begin to wonder how I can help the Lord fulfill His promise to me. This was one of those times. I began to scheme and figure out where I could get this money. The first thought the Devil gave me was, "Why bother the Lord with this when I can raise the money myself by having a King's Teens rally and let the people know of the need?" Surely the Lord would supply the $500 in that way. So I had a rally in the Moore Theatre in downtown Seattle. At offering time I told the people of the need for printing equipment for the expanding King's Teens work and of how the Lord had promised to give us a printing press. We had a fair crowd and a good musical program and I assumed that we would easily net $500. After the rally, when the offering was counted, we discovered that we barely had enough to pay our expenses. I was disheartened and sad as I went home. When I arrived home I immediately went to my bedroom to pray. As I prayed, God gave me afresh the assurance that we still were going to get a printing press from Him, but that He would do it in His own way. I asked the Lord for forgiveness, and He did forgive. "If we confess our sins, He is faithful and just to forgive us our sins, and to cleanse us from all unrighteousness" (I John 1:9). I then waited expectantly for the presses, wondering how He would provide.

About one week later I went downtown and stopped in a small printing shop which belonged to a Mrs. Marie Spidell, in Seattle, to have some printing done. I had never been in her place before. As I came in the door, she said to me, "You are Mike Martin, aren't you?"

I said, "Yes, I am."

She immediately said, "The Lord told me I am to give you my printing equipment."

Surprise, followed by great joy, came into my heart. I thought, of course, that it was the shop I was in but, handing me a piece of paper, she said, "I have another printing shop at this address, and the equipment that the Lord told me to give you for your work is located there." I looked at the address in amazement, for it was the same address where we had looked at the presses on that afternoon when the Holy Spirit had witnessed to us that this was the equipment He was giving us.

I went from there to the other shop and again talked with the man who wanted to sell us Mrs. Spidell's presses. I asked him who owned the presses and he told me Mrs. Spidell did. I had assumed that the presses belonged to him. I then told him I had just seen Mrs. Spidell and she had given us this complete printing shop for King's Teens. Instead of rejoicing with me, the man became angry about it. Perplexed, I left him.

Shortly thereafter a friend of mine told me that he had seen this man and he had accused us of stealing these presses from him. I was shocked to hear this. I went up to see the man alone and, pointing to the presses still in his shop, I asked, "Did you tell people I had stolen these presses from you?"

He hedged a bit but did not say yes or no. I then told him I would go to Mrs. Spidell and get everything straightened up. He said, "No, it's OK I am sorry." I then thought everything was straightened out, but later I heard from other people who had just talked with this printer, and they told me that he had again accusingly said that I had stolen the presses he was using in his shop.

The Word of God says in Matthew 18:15-17, "Moreover if thy brother shall trespass against thee, go and tell him his fault between thee and him alone: if he shall hear thee, thou hast gained thy brother. But if he will not hear thee, then take with thee one or two more, that in the mouth of two or three witnesses every word may be established. And if he shall neglect to hear them, tell it unto the church."

I did this very thing. First I saw him alone, and the second time I went to see him with Marie Spidell and Axel Fredeen, trying to get the matter settled. At the conclusion of the second meeting, again I thought everything was straightened out. He promised not to make any more accusations against us, and he also said that he knew Mrs. Spidell had given the presses to King's Teens. However, a short time later, again I heard he was continuing to circulate this same story. All I could see to do was to follow the instructions in the Bible where it says, "If he will not hear you with two or three witnesses, then bring him before the church." I therefore asked my pastor, Melvin Dahlstrom of the Emanuel Tabernacle in Seattle and a number of Christian businessmen in the city to sit in a church trial to clear me of these accusations concerning these printing presses. I had never before been in or attended a church trial, but I knew this was what the Word of God said to do. Therefore I asked for a church trial and all parties agreed. It was held in the Bible Book Store in Seattle. Mr. Dahlstrom acted as the judge. A number of Christian businessmen acted as a jury for this Christian trial. Mrs. Spidell, the printer who had made these accusations, and I acted as witnesses. When they called on me as a witness I told them that I did not want to take the presses at all unless everything was completely clean and above-board and that I had believed that these presses were the Lord's gift to King's Teens. I put the presses into the hands of these men and said I would not touch this equipment unless they exonerated me completely. Next they called on Mrs. Spidell, and she told how the Lord had spoken to her in the middle of the night and told her she was to give the presses to the King's Teens. The man, when he was called on, said nothing. This trial, of course, completely exonerated me, and the judge and jury gave the presses free and clear to King's Teens. I tried to make friends with the man and tried to shake hands with him, but he did not respond. Some time later, after we had taken the presses to our own shop, I went down to see Mrs. Spidell again, and as I came into her shop, this same printer was visiting with her. I immediately put out my hand and said, "Brother, I want everything to be completely straight between us so that you will love me in the Lord. I have nothing in my heart against you." He would not return my love or make friends with me. I could do nothing else except leave with my heart heavy. When the man left Mrs. Spidell's printing shop just a few minutes later, he fell over dead in the street. I am convinced that the Lord made this last meeting possible in order that we might get every-thing straightened out between us. I sometimes won-der if he would have died had he been willing to make this right. The incident put the fear of the Lord in me in a new way. Oh, that I might not do anything to grieve the Holy Spirit or allow bitterness to come into my heart to hinder the Lord's work in any way.

CHAPTER XVIII

The Birth of King's Garden

During the time I was ill, when God gave us the printing presses, the Lord reminded me again that He had called me out of business and sent me to Bible school for the specific purpose of combating juvenile delinquency through Christianity. I know that Christ is the answer and that there is no other real solution to this problem, for I have seen with my own eyes that when Christ comes into the heart of a teenager, boy or girl, we do not have to worry any longer about juvenile delinquency or whether he will get into trouble with the law. We do need reformatories and the discipline of reformatories for some cases, but the great tragedy is that they leave Christ out, not knowing that He is the only permanent answer, not only to reform but to transform lives, making useful Christians out of former delinquents.

Many teenagers are in difficulty through no fault of their own. So often when parents apply for a divorce, all they think about is who is to get the davenport or chair, the car, and the amount of alimony. They forget what their children are going to do without a father or a mother. As I considered again this great evil of divorce and saw many teenagers who needed help, God asked me to do something about it.

During this time while I was ill, God began to ask me if I would take in boys and girls from broken homes to live with us—teenagers who needed not just a King's Teens meeting but also food, clothing and shelter. Viv and I prayed together, and the Lord told us that He had sent Joanne to our home as a pattern for what He wanted us to do. We believed we had new orders from God as a result of the sickness and fresh revelation from Him. God had already prepared my heart for this work through the following incident.

One day when we were in the midst of our King's Teens work, I had a phone call from a caseworker from the juvenile court who said, "There is a teenage boy here who is in trouble with the law. He said if I could get in touch with you that you would help him out." I immediately went down to see the boy and discovered he was a boy who had attended King's Teens two or three times. He was now charged with theft as a result of stealing some food. I investigated his home environment and found his home a place where they did not even have a kitchen table. They used a big box for a table and smaller boxes to sit on. I discovered that the boy had never had a regular meal, such as meat, potatoes, vegetables, etc., and, being hungry he had gone out to steal some food. His father was ill, and his mother was not a good mother. No regular meals were served. The children got food only when they got to the cupboard first, and there were many times when there was no bread and butter on the shelf. I personally could not condone his stealing, but I have wondered what I would have done as a boy if I were starving. I interceded for this boy and asked the judge to give him into my care. The judge did not want to send this boy to a reformatory. He was sympathetic and was pleased to put the boy into my custody.

Henry Turnidge, my friend who lived on a farm in Oregon, was taking in boys who had difficulty with the law. He too believed that the solution for juvenile delinquency was Christ. I phoned Henry and asked if he would take this boy and help to rehabilitate him on his farm. This he readily agreed to do. The first nine days on the farm, the boy put on a pound a day, or nine pounds in the first nine days. Three months later he came back to his home town and told us how he had found Christ as his personal Savior. The next Sunday he went to church to give his testimony. He asked his mother to come to the meeting to hear him tell of what Christ had done for him. His mother reluctantly came and sat in the back row. As his mother listened to her boy's words, God spoke to her and she too gave her heart to the Lord. In our King's Teens meetings, we met many boys and girls from broken homes and from environments where many needed more than just a meeting. Many needed food, clothing, and shelter. As Viv and I prayed together about this, we came to the conclusion that the Lord wanted us to reach out a helping hand to take in boys and girls from broken homes.

When I was physically strong enough, Viv and I began to look for a place to live where we could take in this type of boy and girl—not especially delinquent children, but rather boys and girls who, through circumstances beyond their control, needed help, home, love, shelter, and—above all—the Lord Jesus Christ. I knew from experience that most of those who became delinquent were from broken homes. Viv and I started to look at farms, expecting to trade our home in on one. It seemed, though, that wherever we went, the doors were closed and the Lord did not indicate to us that any place we looked at was the right one, until one Sunday afternoon in August, 1947. That day a friend had come for dinner. As we visited, I told him about the vision God had given me of taking in boys and girls from broken homes, and I mentioned that there was a large empty place I had heard about, but had not seen—the old Firland Tuberculosis Sanatorium. As we talked about it, we decided to drive out to see it that afternoon. The Sanatorium was located about halfway between Seattle and Everett, at Richmond Highlands. When we arrived we saw a number of large, beautiful buildings—all empty, grass which had grown knee-high, a place which had been abandoned a year before as a result of a much larger U.S. Naval Hospital being offered to them free of charge. As we looked around the 53 acres of land and 35 buildings, the thought came to us, "This is so big. How can it be possible to claim so large a place for the Lord?"

After we had driven around the place, we decided to get out of the car and start walking, and as we walked, the Lord began to speak to my heart. After a while we stopped at a tree near a large building which we call the Nightingale (now Ambassador) Building. I said to my friend and to my wife, "Let us kneel here and pray, asking God if He would have us claim this place for Him." As the three of us prayed, the Lord spoke to me, reminding me of the scripture in Joshua 1:3 which reads, "Every place that the sole of your foot shall tread upon, that have I given unto you, as I said unto Moses." When we finished praying, I told the others, "The Lord spoke to me and told me that wherever the sole of my foot shall tread, He will give to us. Therefore, I am going to take this verse literally, and I am going to walk around this place barefooted and claim this place for God." I then took off my shoes and socks and walked around the place barefoot, claiming it for the Lord. It looked queer, I know, to see a grown man in his forties walking barefooted, but I am so thankful the Lord honors His word when we act upon it. When we came home after that visit, I felt I needed further assurance from God, and on my knees in my bedroom I told the Lord, "I am claiming this place for you, but I need to be positively sure that this is Your will. Would You please give me a verse of scripture so that I will know that this is what You want me to do." I opened my Bible and glanced down, and these verses in Jeremiah 32:26, 27, and 28a, seemed to jump right out of the Bible into my heart. "Then came the word of the Lord unto Jeremiah, saying, Behold, I am the Lord, the God of all flesh: is there anything too hard for me? Therefore thus saith the Lord; Behold, I will give this city."

As I read that, the Lord made this real to my heart and I knew for sure He was going to give us the old Firland Tuberculosis Sanatorium, now King's Garden. I took my Bible and scratched out Jeremiah's name and inserted my name, so that it now reads in my Bible, "Then came the word of the Lord unto Mike Martin, saying, Behold, I am the Lord, the God of all flesh: is there anything too hard for me? Therefore, thus saith the Lord; Behold, I will give this city." I call this God's deed to the King's Garden.

The purpose of this book is to help you to see that the age of miracles has not passed away. I have put down with pen and ink some of the many miracles that the Lord has done for us. "Jesus Christ is the same yesterday, and today, and forever" (Hebrews 13:8). The Lord is no respecter of persons, and that which He did for us, He did also for our other full-time King's Teen workers who also "lived by faith." As our King's Teens work expanded, we saw the need of having additional workers, working full time in other places. In response to prayer, the Lord sent us a number of wonderful full-time workers. The first was Ednalee Lewis, who assisted us in Seattle. Secondly there were Earnest and Henrietta Fells, who were in charge of the state of Oregon. Third were Bob and Dorothy Reese, who took charge of the clubs in eastern Washington. Then came David and Beulah Sheridan, who also worked with us in the Seattle area.

The Lord can and He did provide all their needs in answer to prayer, even as He did for Viv and me, but throughout the world there are people even as we, who have proved the Lord in "living by faith." It is impossible in this book to tell the miracle stories of these dear people or of the hundreds of adult counselors who operated their individual King's Teens Clubs.

I have given you only some of the events and miracles that God used to prepare my heart for the next big task of taking in boys and girls from broken homes at King's Garden, plus being the founder of schools, radio stations, a printing establishment, rest homes, correctional schools, Christian resorts, mission services, etc., at the King's Garden and other places. If I had attempted to tell all that the Lord has done for me and the many miracles I have witnessed, this book would be endless.

In a future book which we will entitle the King's Garden, we will tell the miracle story of King's Garden, of how God gave us this beautiful place, 53 acres of land and its 35 buildings, for just one dollar a year, in order for us to do this new work He had called us to, that of helping boys and girls from broken homes.

"The Lord spoke to me and told me that wherever the sole of my foot shall tread, He will give to us."
— Mike Martin

The three children of Mike and Vivian; Curtis, Joyce, and Michael stand in front of the administration building.

"I am convinced that no work of God can carry on without those who will help carry the load in prayer and that God does nothing except in answer to prayer."
—Mike Martin

First class entertainment at a King's Teens event in 1954.

King's Teens began in the Martin home at 6059 Sycamore Avenue.

The annual King's Teens Valentine Banquet was not only a wonderful evening of fine dining and great entertainment, it was an avenue for hundreds to come to belief in Christ.

King's Garden Buys Old Firland Site for $100,001!
"After the auction Martin told the crowd that the credit
for King's Garden retaining the site goes 'to the Lord
Jesus Christ.'"—Seattle Times, Monday April 14, 1958.

The 1958 Victory Banquet celebrating the purchase of the Firland property by King's Garden. The verse on the banner is a portion of Jeremiah 32:26—the "deed to King's Garden."

Beginning in 1956, a tent was erected on the grounds
to house the annual missionary rally. The King's Garden Missions Department's slogan was "A missionary
to the missionaries."

Joanne Paping. "I believe that if we had not taken Joanne in, the Lord would not have given us the opportunity of helping others, nor would He have given us King's Garden."
—Mike Martin

"The Cabin" located near Mike Martin Gym, has been home to many King's Garden and CRISTA workers over the years.

Aerial view of Firland Sanatorium at the time that it became King's Garden.

Monroe Johnston, Kathryn Boomer, Pauline (Swaney) Johnston, and Elta DeBruyn operate a print shop on the grounds. King's Press met the printing needs of King's Garden as well as providing missionary literature in many foreign languages.

Mike Martin was a man of God who believed in God's promises. His great burden for young people, sensitivity to God's leading, and boldness through faith is ever producing fruit from one generation to the next.

Vivian Martin was the beloved wife of Mike Martin and faithful chronicler of the miraculous events that surrounded the beginnings of King's Garden.

Accomplished By Faith

CHAPTER I

The Lord God Planted a Garden

"Ye have not chosen me but I have chosen you"
John 15:16

"Going once, going twice. . . Is no one else going to bid? Sold to the King's Garden for $100,001."

To understand the above words called out by the auctioneer, walk with me down Memory Lane, and let me tell you a story of God's faithfulness to a man who dared to trust Him for great things. That man was my husband whose real name was Alvin B. Martin, but was known by the nickname of "Mike" for most of his life. God used him to found the organization of King's Garden which is located in the suburbs north of Seattle, Washington.

I think the best place to begin my story is one warm, lazy August, Sunday afternoon in 1948. We had had a guest speaker in our church that morning and had brought him home with us to share our Sunday dinner. As it was quite warm during the afternoon, we sat out on the lawn to cool off. We talked of many trivial things, and then my husband began to speak of the thought dearest to his heart—starting a home for boys and girls.

We had been working among teenagers in his school club work, and had seen boys and girls who needed more than just a weekly meeting; they needed a home and love. As he told of this dream, we discovered our guest had the same interest, and we talked together about where such a place could be started, and how the finances could be obtained.

Mike and I had been hunting for a farm to buy that summer, thinking perhaps we could trade our home as a down-payment, and so have room enough to take in a few teenagers to live with us. We had taken one girl into our own home and she had grown as dear to us as our own children. She found the Lord as her Savior just a few days after she came to us and lived with us until she graduated from high school. Then she attended Bible school and later married a Christian man. We could see from her life what could be accomplished in the lives of teenagers, but we knew we would need a larger home before we could make a home for more young people.

Finally Mike began to think aloud and said, "I know where there is a place which is vacant, but it is so large. I wonder . . ." His voice trailed off, and then he suggested, "At least let us drive out and look at it."

We got into our car and drove out to the old sanatorium. It was large and beautiful, but dreadfully neglected. The entrance to old Firland, the future King's Garden, was a long avenue, lined on each side with huge poplar trees. The drive led straight to a large, regal-looking administration building of Tudor architecture with a crown-like dome, topped with the double-barred Anti-Tuberculosis cross. As we faced this building, to the left was a 252-foot long sanatorium hospital three stories high, and behind this was what had been a hospital for children. Half-way down the drive was another large cream-colored building.

In addition to these large structures, there were several small ones; a store, a cabin, several miscellaneous buildings and a farm, where the sanatorium had raised pigs and chickens for their own use. Besides this, there was a power-house with boilers for heating the whole institution, but of course these had not been in operation for some time. All this was situated on 42 acres of land, of which about 12 acres was in lawn. However, the lawn had not been cared for and it had grown almost to our knees. Many varieties of trees, shrubs, and flowers had been planted in abundance, and predominate were the fir trees, from which Firland had received its name. This property had been appraised at two million dollars.

After driving for awhile we stopped the car and knelt under one of the fir trees. We asked the Lord what His will was for us. As I knelt there, I had the strangest feeling that God was telling me this was the place He had selected for our home for teenagers. I do not remember even arguing with the Lord about it, but rather being paralyzed with fright at the thoughts which were coming to me.

Suddenly, to my amazement, Mike got to his feet and said, "The Lord just told me that wherever the sole of my feet will tread upon, He will give me. I am going to take the Lord up on this and walk around this place, claiming it for Him." He reached down to take off his shoes and stockings, explaining he felt it meant the sole of his feet and not the sole of his shoes, and we began to walk around that large institution. As we walked, Mike was talking aloud to the Lord, "Lord, You can see that I am walking around this place claiming it for you, even as You told me." The conviction was in my heart that we had found God's will, but Mike was still a little hesitant on the way home. I think he could see, better than I, the magnitude of the job ahead of us.

Mike now went up into our bedroom to be alone with the Lord. We were still young in our Christian experience. (The story of our conversion is told in Mike's book, *I Live By Faith*.) We were delving in the Word, but we still had much to learn. Mike did not even know that God had spoken directly to him through His Word as found in Joshua 1:3. He asked the Lord to give him a definite promise from the Word, so that he would know this was the home God would give us. It was at this time God gave him Jeremiah 32:26, 27 and 28, which was to play such a big part in our future:

"Then came the Word of the Lord unto Jeremiah, saying, 'Behold I am the Lord, the God of all flesh; is there anything too hard for me?' Therefore, thus saith the Lord, 'Behold, I will give this city . . . .'"

Mike crossed out Jeremiah's name and inserted his own name, for the promise was to him, personally. Later on, after King's Garden had received its name, Mike wrote in the margin of his Bible, "This is the deed to the King's Garden."

Five years before this, we had started a young people's club in our home which we named King's Teens. Teenagers enjoyed coming to our home on Tuesday evenings for a time of singing, Bible study and fellowship.

As time went on others too desired to have a club in their home and at the time Mike received this promise from Jeremiah, there were hundreds of teenagers meeting in homes in the northwest area and there even were a few clubs in other states.

Sometime during 1947, Mike had felt that the work of King's Teens should be incorporated. This was before we had been called to start a home for boys and girls from broken homes. I am sure it was under the inspiration of the Holy Spirit that he listed the various ministries as he did. Following is a paragraph copied from the incorporation papers:

a. To engage in, foster, encourage, promote, and propagate evangelical churches and missions, and Christian charitable interests, including establishment, maintenance, and operation of orphanages, homes for juveniles and others, hospitals, and schools in this state and throughout the world.

b. To use every method such as radio, television, pictures, literature, and the spoken word, etc., that the people of the world may hear the gospel and accept Christ as their own personal Savior. All work of this Corporation shall be of an interdenominational character, and no discrimination shall be shown to anyone regardless of their race, creed, or nationality.

This incorporation was approved before our application to lease old Firland Sanatorium was made.

Later, when opposition to our obtaining this lease arose, one of the supervisors in the government wrote to Mike as follows:

"This is to advise you that we are closing our records concerning King's Teens since we are assuming that plans are not going forward, as no written application has been received from the proposed incorporators. We have advised the Secretary of State that King's, Inc., also known as King's Teens, has not been approved for operation of a children's agency."

When Mike received this letter, he wrote to this individual that we were already incorporated and would not need further incorporation. Later Mike received a letter reading, "I am sorry to inform you that you are incorporated. I was on my vacation when your application came through and it was approved in my absence." This incorporation, which God so miraculously put through by sending the one who would be opposed on a vacation, kept us from having any further trouble along this line. Since it was so complete, we did not have to seek any further incorporation as the other ministries were added, one by one.

King's Teens had a small board and the first thing Mike did after receiving this promise about Firland, was to call a meeting and tell them how the Lord had been dealing with us, and that he felt he should make application to lease the old Firland Sanatorium. The Board members desired to see the place Mike had in mind, and it was my privilege to go with them the day they went out to see the site. Mike obtained the help of a caretaker so that we could enter the buildings and see what the inside of them looked like. We were overwhelmed at the immensity of the buildings and we also discovered that all of the major buildings were joined by underground tunnels, so people could go from one building to the next through them.

After walking for quite a period of time and viewing the many buildings and grounds, we found our way down to a small park. In this park we found a small cabin which we entered. We all knelt in prayer, asking the Lord to reveal His will. As we were praying, the Holy Spirit witnessed to each one that this was the location He was going to give us. This park was a part of old Firland and later was named "The Garden of Prayer."

A few days later, Mike called another meeting—a day of fasting and prayer—for many matters needed to be settled, and one of the most important was the finances. God spoke to both Mike and me during this day, asking us if we were willing to give our home and all that we had to see our dream of having a home for boys and girls become a reality. We renewed the pledge we had made previously of complete surrender. We then felt the Lord gave us the courage which we needed to begin the work of acquiring this property for Him. What to re-name Firland was also given consideration at this meeting. One morning while praying, Axel Fredeen, the Vice-President of the Board, had been given the name, "King's Garden." When he told the Board of the name he had been given in prayer it seemed so exactly right, for even though the premises were unkempt and run down, we could envision what it could become.

Mike went down to the government offices in Seattle to inquire what steps to take in order to make application to lease the property and was referred to the Tuberculosis Board of Managers who were in charge of the place. Mr. James Mifflin was President of this board, and he was wonderfully cooperative and encouraged Mike to try to secure Firland for God. He, too, was interested in helping boys and girls from broken homes. Mike received encouragement from all the officials with whom he talked, but of course it was necessary for them to approach the matter in a businesslike way. "How can it be financed?" they kept asking dubiously.

After getting all the information he could on how to proceed, Mike called another meeting of the King's Teens Board and together they discussed how much money they should offer to pay to lease the property. The sum agreed upon was $500 per month. Mike also contacted people who knew of the work of King's Teens and asked for references from them. Many were willing to help, and he soon had a whole sheaf of letters, confirming that King's Teens was a worthwhile work and should be given serious consideration.

A letter was sent out to our friends, acquainting people with our desire to secure the old Firland Sanatorium to start a home for teenagers. We requested prayer and asked for contributions. To our delight $1,500 came in as a result.

Mike gathered up all the references he had received, and went down to make formal application to lease the old Firland Sanatorium for $500 per month. The county commissioners, having received several other applications to lease or buy this property, appointed a committee composed of various heads of institutions and organizations. They were to interview each applicant and to choose one to whom the place might be leased or sold.

When Mike's turn came to be interviewed, he was placed in the center of a circle of men. Their questions rained over him.

"How much education do you have?" Mike had only a high school education plus three years of Bible school. When he told them of his Bible school training he was told Bible school could not be considered as education.

"How much training have you had in running an institution?" Mike had to admit he had none.

"How much money do you have to operate an institution of this size?" Since we had been living by faith, simply trusting the Lord to send in money for our needs, he probably had only one or two dollars in his pocket. This would represent our total cash, since we did not have a bank account.

He shuddered to tell them he had nothing, so he said truthfully, "Not very much."

Then they asked the final question, "Then what do you have?" This was Mike's opportunity. He opened his Bible to Jeremiah 32, and read the promise he had been given. The committee instantly dismissed him.

A few days later Mike received a copy of a letter which the committee had sent to the county commissioners. It was very uncomplimentary and said, "These people are ignorant, untrained people. It would be better to let the place go to rack and ruin than to lease it to them."

Upon receiving this letter, Mike was quite shocked for he had been trusting the Lord to work miracles so the home for boys and girls could be started. However, as was his custom when in need, he went to the only Person he knew who could help him. He fled to his room, knelt down beside the bed, with his Bible and the letter in his hand. He wept as he told the Lord that he had relied upon His promise. What could this letter of refusal mean? Hardly knowing what he was doing, he opened his Bible and to his surprise it opened to Jeremiah: the same promise. Mike exclaimed joyfully, "Lord, the promise is still there! It has not changed! What is wrong?" Then the Lord began to show him that getting all the recommendations was wrong, and that the offer of $500 a month was also wrong.

"Forgive me, Lord, and show me what to do and I promise to obey you." was Mike's earnest prayer.

The Lord replied, "Withdraw the offer of $500 a month rent and offer $1 a year instead, and do not use any recommendations. I am all the recommendation you need."

The next day Mike went back to Mr. Mifflin to tell him he was going to apply all over again. Mr. Mifflin was still sympathetic and said, "Fine, Mike, what are you going to offer this time?"

Mike's reply was, "$1 a year." Mr. Mifflin must have been taken aback with such an unexpected reply, but still he encouraged Mike to do as he felt led, "Atta boy, Mike, keep trying!"

CHAPTER II

The Steps of a Good Man

"The steps of a good man are ordered by the Lord..."
Psalm 37:23

Mike started with God's way this time, and followed His explicit instructions from day to day. Mike needed only to be alone with the Lord long enough for him to hear His voice and follow what He told him. I can remember that Mike spent many hours alone in prayer, sometimes praying the entire night. Each day he would pray, "What do you want me to do today?" Then he would go out on whatever errand the Lord sent him. Hundreds of visits were made to various public officials, to people who would pray for this project, and to people who would help financially. Mike also spent much time in prayer with other men for this project.

Every Monday evening he attended a prayer meeting held in the basement of The Beanery, a small school store across the street from a high school. These prayer meetings were attended by two or three men and often would continue the entire night. On Tuesday evening he frequently attended a prayer meeting in downtown Seattle directed by Axel Fredeen. These men helped to bear the burden with Mike and were of great encouragement to him.

Approximately six months after the time of receiving the first refusal, the county commissioners held another hearing in their offices. They had not been able to decide who should have old Firland. Many people had endeavored to obtain it. Large sums of money had been offered.

The commissioners faced some very real problems about the matter. The Firland property originally had been given as a gift to the city of Seattle to be used for tuberculosis purposes. The city of Seattle in turn had given the property to the county with the stipulation that it must be used for tuberculosis purposes only. Otherwise, Firland should be sold and the money used for the work at new Firland. Firland had moved to the old naval hospital after the war was over and the name of Firland was continued for the new location. However, the Firland administration was not sure if this was a permanent move, thinking perhaps they might wish to move back to old Firland at some future date. Until a firm decision was made, the county commissioners were prohibited from selling the institution.

The commissioners gave Mike an opportunity to speak at this hearing. He told the story of how God had called him out of business to combat juvenile delinquency through Christianity, and that we were ministering to over 1,500 young people in club meetings held in homes once a week. He told of the boys and girls we had come in contact with who were from broken homes and needed more than just a weekly club meeting. He told them we felt if we could be at the head of the stream we could save these young people from falling into trouble and in this way would save the county thousands of dollars. As Mike explained all this and read them the promise they saw his sincerity. This was during the spring of 1949.

We lived from day to day in great expectancy; we thought that the Lord was going to deliver old Firland to us at any time. Mike was so sure of it, he felt he was already living there. He greatly embarrassed me one evening at prayer meeting by giving a testimony in which he thanked the Lord for the privilege of living at King's Garden. After the service, people came to us and asked, "Is it true that you are living at King's Garden?" It was only then that Mike realized what he had said in his testimony. He was not really living at King's Garden. Only his heart was there!

Since we had promised the Lord our home, we put it up for sale that spring. We asked God to control the time of selling so that we would not be left without a place to live. No one even came to look at it until July when a buyer came. We felt that God was testing our faith to see if we were willing to step out and trust Him explicitly in the matter of leasing Firland. We signed the papers for selling our home. Now we had only 30 days before we had to move.

One day Mike paid a visit to the man who was a member of the Tuberculosis Board of Managers. He asked Mike how he planned to finance the work. When Mike told him, "The Lord will provide," he demanded proof. He asked that Mike bring him the equivalent of $30,000, either in cash, bonds, or deeds to property, and put it on his desk on Friday morning. Since this was on Wednesday, it became a real test of Mike's faith. Axel Fredeen was with Mike that morning. Together they went into a restaurant and ordered cups of coffee. Then they prayed, "Lord, if the lease of old Firland is to be a reality, it will be necessary to bring down $30,000 to prove that we are able to handle the finances. We desperately need your help."

There had been several people who had indicated an interest in our project. They had told Mike that when a lease would be forthcoming they would be willing to invest some money in the King's Garden. After prayer, the men separated and Mike began to call on these people with good results. By Thursday evening Mike had $22,000 in checks, bonds and deeds. This left $8,000 still to be secured and time was running out. God brought to Mike's memory a couple who lived on an island. They had mentioned sometime before that they were interested, and desired to invest some money when it was needed.

Mike called them long distance that evening. This, in substance, is what the lady told him on the phone, in answer to Mike's query: "Yes, Mike, we are interested in helping and we had thought of putting $5,000 into the project, but the Lord seems to be indicating that it should be $8,000 instead." Mike then told her this was just the amount he still needed, and that it was necessary to have it by the next morning, so they sent the necessary papers over posthaste by special messenger.

Friday morning Mike went down and laid the assets on the desk. The board member then returned them saying, "I just wanted to make sure you could handle such a large undertaking. You don't need to leave the assets with me." To make this matter still more amazing, just a few days later, one man who had contributed $5,000 wrote and asked for his money back, saying he needed it. One by one, for one reason or another, the others asked for return of their investment. When the time came for us to move to the King's Garden, our assets were only the original $1,500 which had come in through small contributions as a result of the circular letter. Even the money from the sale of our home which was to be largely used in the project, was not forthcoming until sometime in November.

After selling our home, Mike went to the commissioners and asked if we might not go out to Firland and start cleaning while they were considering what to do. They gave their permission for us to go out at our own risk to mow the lawns and start cleaning the buildings. However, they really did not intend for us to move out there, but only to work out there in the daytime. Mike did not understand this and took it as permission to move to King's Garden.

The Lord dealt much with my own heart in those days, for I faced the future with much fear. I began to think how terrible it would be if no one came to help us with the work. Immediately the Lord asked me, "Are you willing to move out alone with your family, if no one else comes?" Before I received peace on this matter I had to promise the Lord that I was willing to move out there all alone, if that was His will. It was of great concern to me though, for I knew I would be afraid to be in the administration building all alone when Mike was gone so often in the evenings. I spent much time, too, in wondering, "What will we do with all that space?" I remember telling Mike I thought we could make use of half of the administration building, but whatever would we do with all the rest? I had no vision at all of the great task ahead of us and what King's Garden was to become. How thankful I am that God leads us gently step by step and does not give us more than we can stand at one time.

CHAPTER III

He Brought Me Forth

"He brought me forth also into a large place."
II Samuel 22 :20

Mike had been jubilant when he returned home from talking with the county commissioners, for he thought he had permission to move out to the King's Garden and start to work, even though we still did not have a lease. This was not a concern to him, for he felt this was only another testing of his faith. He was willing to step out on the promise of God that He would "give the city." Of course if the county should lease the place to someone else, we would lose all the money invested, and also the labor of cleaning and renovating.

Because there were still two weeks before we had to move out of our home, we decided to wait there as long as possible and use our home as a base for operations. For those two weeks Mike drove out to the property in the mornings and returned home in the evenings to sleep. I stayed at home to do the office work and get our packing done. A young couple who had indicated a desire to help us, moved out first, to guard the place, and begin to get things somewhat cleaned for other workers who would be coming in soon.

One of the first gifts we received was 500 chickens. This was a very welcome one for they supplied eggs for our needs. By the time our family moved out to King's Garden on August 15, there was a small colony of families living there and working with all their might. It was a real sacrifice for them to leave their means of livelihood and move to the King's Garden, trusting the Lord for their needs. We could only promise them their room and board and a small allowance as the Lord provided for it. It was a real blessing to both Mike and me to see their willingness to come under those circumstances.

The day we moved out there, the Lord gave Mike the song, "I have decided to follow Jesus," and he was singing lustily as we drove along. This song continued to be his dedication song and has often been sung by the workers.

At first the only means of cooking for the workers was a hot plate, and the only place where there was any hot water was in the store building. This necessitated carrying buckets of water for about a block. We all ate together in the one dining room.

When people saw that we had actually moved to the King's Garden and were working there, volunteers came in droves to help with the gigantic task of cleaning. We had been told that since this had been a tuberculosis sanatorium, it would be best if all the walls were washed with soap and water. One of the great needs was rags to wash the walls with. We asked those who came to wash, to bring all the rags they could, but soon these were all used up. Rags cost $6 a bale in those days and we did not feel we could take our few precious funds to purchase any. So we held a prayer meeting and the next day one of our workers was walking in the tunnels. There were small rooms off these tunnels and he glanced into one as he walked by. His eyes fell on six bales of rags, clean and ready to be used. He came running to Mike about his find. Together they praised the Lord for this provision.

The main kitchen was in bad condition. There was a fungus growth on the walls, which looked like hair and was approximately two to three inches in length. When the door was opened, the hairs would wave in the breeze. The men took a garden hoe, scraped the walls and then started to wash them. The kitchen range had about one-half inch of scum on the top of it. An electric buffer was used to take this off and it took three days to get down to the metal. After ten days the kitchen was all clean. There was great rejoicing when the stove was ready to be used, and we began to have the use of the ovens, so that preparing the food was an easier task.

Among the earliest workers was an elderly retired baker and his wife. I will never forget the long, luscious loaves of bread which he baked in great quantity. Whenever we had guests visiting King's Garden, the exclamations over the delicious bread were many.

Next, attention was turned to the water supply. The water department was asked to turn on the water in the main buildings. It was then we found out for the first time that Firland had forgotten to turn off the water when they moved, and the water, instead of coming out through faucets, came out from the walls in the places where the pipes were broken. All they could do was to turn on the water and station men with pipe wrenches and axes in various places. As the breaks were found, these men would chop into the wall and repair the pipe. It took a number of days of this kind of work to get the water coming through the pipes in the right way. Often when water spurted from the wall, some of the women washing on the walls would get a soaking.

Another difficult problem was that most of the tile on the floors had buckled and it was necessary to pry it all off and lay new tile. These were great tasks for such a small crew of men workers, but they all worked tremendously hard and hours were forgotten in their eagerness to see the work accomplished. It was damp and cold in the buildings because the heat had not yet been turned on but it was a real blessing that the fall was such a warm one. The sun shone brightly practically every day, which made the work much easier. When people would comment on the beautiful fall weather, we would answer that God had given such nice weather because there was no heat in the buildings.

We were so happy at the King's Garden and eager to share our joy with other people. We decided to hold a rally on the lawn the last Sunday afternoon in August. We invited people to come out and see what we were doing and to take a tour of the buildings and grounds. It was a beautiful warm day and a great crowd came. The Salvation Army Band played several numbers, and then Mike gave a short talk on what we desired to do at King's Garden. One of the county commissioners came, and when he heard we were living there, he became quite alarmed. He told Mike the County had not intended for us to move out to Firland and it would be tragic if the place should be leased to someone else now.

Mike only continued to witness to him and to all others, that God was going to perform the miracle and that old Firland was going to be leased to us. Since we were banking on God's promise we did not feel there was any risk.

Finally as colder weather began to come, it was decided the boilers should be turned on. One of our first workers told Mike he could operate boilers, but that he did not understand how to get them ready for operation and would need some help. So the two of them prayed together, and George prayed something like this, "Lord, send us a man to start the boilers, one who is well experienced, an older man, one sort of fat and jolly." This prayer stayed in Mike's mind for he thought it was a very unusual prayer.

One Saturday evening, Mike and I went to Youth for Christ. After the service a man came up to us and said, "Do you need an engineer out at your place? I am one." He was an older man, heavy set and happy looking. We could see he fit the description of the man George had prayed for. He moved to the Garden and we found indeed he knew how to fix boilers. It was only a short time before the boilers were ready for operation. We had been told many times that it would cost $1,500 to put the boilers into operation and we knew that our small bank balance would not permit any such expenditure.

When the engineer came asking about buying oil he told Mike it would take a lot and would cost quite a sum of money. Mike told him we had so little money he did not feel we could use all we had to buy oil. They prayed together and asked the Lord what to do. Some days later as one of the men was cleaning behind the power house he found an oil tank which no one knew was there. He came in and got a stick to measure the oil. He found there were 6,000 gallons in the tank. People would ask, "Was the oil there before?" Mike always answered he did not know, but he liked to think it was the same as the cruse of oil mentioned in the Old Testament, that the Lord just poured it in. When the time came for starting up the boilers, the only cost was for some wood to start the fire burning.

However, after the boilers were turned on, an unexpected catastrophe happened. A large thermostatic valve split down the middle because it had not been used for so long. Again the boilers were shut down, and again the men prayed. The engineer inquired over the phone about the cost of a valve. He was told there was none available in the northwest. It would be necessary to order one from the east. The price would be between $300 to $400. The men were rather downcast over this news. Aimlessly, one began to rummage around, under the benches. It was there he found a valve just like the one which was broken; a brand new one which was still in its wrappings. You can imagine the rejoicing there was over this answer to prayer!

We still had many needs, and one of the most necessary was some means of communication between the buildings. The intercommunication system which was left when Firland moved, was not in working order. This was a real trial, as we were few in number and the buildings were large and covered quite an area. When a person was needed, it was necessary to send some one to find him. This often took quite a period of time and when it was an emergency, it was quite a trial. We began to pray for this need and asked God to send someone to fix the intercommunication system. Two weeks later a man contacted Mike. He asked if we needed some electricians to help us get things started. He said there were some men working in the Navy yard in Bremerton who were desirous of helping if there was anything they could do. When Mike told him of our need, he brought five or six men over on Friday evening after their work at the yard was over. They worked all night Friday, all day Saturday, and then they returned home. On the following weekend they came again and on the third weekend they completed the work so that the system could be used. This was a real blessing and time-saver.

These electricians continued to help when they could and next started to work on the electrical system. One day Mike was walking on the avenue, and saw an electrician searching for a short circuit in the wiring for the lamp posts. The man told Mike he had been hunting for this short for several hours. Mike told him, "I know how to find it."

Greatly amazed, he asked, "How?"

Mike told him they should pray and the Lord would help him find it. So the two of them bowed their heads and asked God to reveal to the electrician where the short was so that it could be speedily repaired.

Mike walked on and later came back over the same path. As he neared the workman, the man shouted, "It works, Mike, prayer works! We found the short!" One of Mike's favorite sayings was, "Prayer is the greatest time-saver of all."

God gave our workers love for one another, for we were just as a big family and when anything happened, it affected us all. One day a little girl belonging to a worker's family was lost. We looked and shouted, but no little girl. Finally, one of the men said he thought he remembered seeing her, and that she had purple stain on her lips. We became very alarmed, because, when the staff of old Firland had moved, many things were left behind including medicine and various chemicals, and we still had not had the opportunity to clean them all out. We gathered together at the front of the administration building and pleaded with the Lord to help us find the child. Finally the mother returned to their living quarters and found her daughter asleep in her own bed. Her lips did have a purple stain on them, but evidently she had not swallowed anything harmful.

We were so dependent on the Lord in those early days. A few contributions were coming in, enough to supply our food and other necessary expenses, but we continued to have needs which our limited funds could not supply. It was very interesting to see the many different ways God used to meet our needs. One of these was for a truck. One day a man called Mike on the phone and told him he was buying a new truck and instead of turning in his old truck on the new one, he would like to offer it to King's Garden. He hesitated to give it because it did not have a truck bed. However, Mike assured him we had a great need for a truck and we would get along with its use even though it did not have a bed.

When the truck was delivered, the men remembered there was a truck bed near the farm buildings. When they checked, they found it was the exact size to fit on the truck.

One day a photographer offered to make a movie for us showing the story of how the King's Garden was started, and we were very glad to accept his offer. It was very interesting to me to see the various scenes being made and to have a small part in it. One problem I continually faced was about my hair. I wanted it to look nice in the pictures so whenever they told me they would be shooting some scenes that day, I would find someone who would dress my hair. Then later I might be told the scenes could not be made that day. Again when I was least expecting it, I would be informed, "We will be shooting pictures in a few minutes." My lament was always, "But my hair! What about my hair?" Another amusing aspect to the making of this film was our car which had one dented fender. It took a lot of maneuvering to keep the dent from being noticeable when it was filmed. When it was finished we found this film was a great help in presenting the work of King's Garden everywhere.

CHAPTER IV

Pray Without Ceasing

"Pray without ceasing . . ."
I Thessalonians 5:17

Before I go any further with my story, let me go back to the time before we moved to King's Garden to pick up the threads of another portion of my narrative.

When we sent out the first circular letter, telling people the Lord had promised to give us the old Firland Sanatorium and asking people to pray and to give, one of the letters found its way to the home of Cappy Frisbie. She had been ill for some time. Several years before this Mrs. Frisbie had a cerebral hemorrhage and had been in bed for a long period of time. She began to listen to her radio, and one day she gave her heart to the Lord after listening to a gospel message. She began to get well and witness for the Lord in many places. However, later on she had a relapse, and became partially paralyzed once more.

One day shortly before our circular letter went out, she had been listening to her radio. She heard a voice asking those who were listening to surrender their lives to the Lord and give all to Him; anything the Lord asked of them. This dear lady made a commitment to the Lord and told Him He could have anything she had. The morning our letter came to her, the Lord began to reveal to her that since she had surrendered her life to Him, she should accept that which He sent to her. He also told her that the letter which had come and which she had carelessly tossed into the wastebasket without opening, was something He wanted her to read, that He had caused it to be sent to her. She went to the basket and took out the letter and read it. The Lord then asked if He could have her home and use the money to help start the work of King's Garden. He told her that He would cure her paralysis when she had given her home.

Since she was not completely confined to her bed, she went to the phone and called Mike and asked him to come over to see her. When he came, he saw that Mrs. Frisbie was partially paralyzed. She was clad in pajamas and her hair hung in long braids. Her home was beautiful, built on the edge of a lake. She told him her story and that she was supposed to give her home to King's Teens to help start the old Firland project. She told him that the Lord had promised to heal her body when the house was given. Mike was very fearful and told her we could not take her home until he had permission from the corporate board. He promised her that the board members would pray and seek to find God's will in the matter.

After much prayer and several meetings, the board members went to see Mrs. Frisbie to reason with her, but she kept insisting that we must take her home so that she could be healed. Shortly before we moved to the Garden, before her home was given, Mrs. Frisbie asked if we would take her out to see King's Garden.

Mike and I, and two others, went over to her home and helped her into our car.

On the way out there, she became very ill and began to vomit. We were all distressed at her suffering and wanted to turn around and take her home again. She kept insisting that she wanted to continue on for she was determined to see the place she was to help start. We all felt the opposition of the Devil. We were afraid she might die. Then people would say we were taking advantage of one who was ill.

Finally we got to the entrance of King's Garden, but then she was too ill to even raise her head to see anything. We got out of the car and walked around it, praying for Mrs. Frisbie and for protection. It was a very real spiritual battle. We then called for an ambulance to come and soon she was home in her own bed once more, none the worse for the experience.

The day finally came when the King's Garden board members decided it must be the will of the Lord to accept the gift of this home and that it was His provision for the work of King's Garden. Just before we moved out there, Mike told her we would sign the papers accepting this gift. She was very joyful at this news. Mike and the secretary of the board went downtown one morning and had all the necessary papers made out and signed for the transfer of this property. Then Mike went alone to tell Mrs. Frisbie that the transfer was completed.

When he got to her home, he expected to go in and tell her the news in her house. Instead she saw Mike coming. When the car stopped, she ran out and jumped into the car. She was completely recovered from her paralysis. She told him, "I feel just like a gazelle." Mike did not know what a gazelle was, but he did not like to admit that. When he came back to our home he looked the word up in the dictionary. The definition: "Any of various small antelopes of Africa, Near East, and Asia." In other words, she felt light and graceful. When they compared the time when the papers were signed and when she was healed, they found it was exactly at the same time. What a tremendous miracle!

It took a few weeks before her home was sold and the money was not available for use until about the end of November. She also turned in her insurance policies and gave that money to King's Garden. A short time later she moved into a small cabin on the grounds. She told me she felt that the Lord was calling her to a ministry of prayer. She prayed practically all day long for the different ministries, and one of her major ministries was to pray for Mike that he would have the wisdom to make the right decisions as they came up. Often when Mike was facing a hard problem and did not know what to do, he would go to Cappy and pray with her.

One day Mike was feeling depressed because Christian people were severely criticizing him for starting King's Garden. He went down to pray with Cappy. He thought Cappy would sympathize with him, but instead she asked sharply, "Mike, are you counting this all joy?" It was a real lesson for Mike and he never did forget it. From then on he tried to count any hard trial which came his way as "all joy."

Other workers too, when they needed spiritual help, would wend their way to Cappy's little cabin and there they found the encouragement and help they needed. For a few years, too, she walked around the Garden daily and looked for those workers who seemed to be discouraged and would ask them to pray with her. A few times when Mike told her of some ministry the Lord seemed to be leading him into, she would simply say, "I prayed for that to happen years ago."

Cappy is home with the Lord now, and the last few years of her life were spent in much suffering. Even then she would pray much for the work. Only eternity will reveal all that Cappy accomplished through prayer. I know that her reward in heaven is great. Hers was a completely dedicated life, and I know King's Garden would not have come into being if it had not been for Cappy's complete obedience to the Lord. The fragrance of her spirit-filled life will always linger at the King's Garden. I know she had "an abundant entrance into the everlasting kingdom of the Lord" when she went to be with Him in 1960.

CHAPTER V

He That Winneth Souls

" . . . And he that winneth souls is wise."
Proverbs 11:30

Two of our ministries were started before we moved to the King's Garden. One of these was the King's Teens work, the high school clubs mentioned in the first chapter. Headquarters for this work was transferred to King's Garden shortly after we moved there.

At about the same time, it became apparent Mike could not carry on the work of King's Teens in addition to handling the work of King's Garden. God wonderfully provided leaders for this work. Our own daughter first worked in this department. Next to come was Juanita Berg who handled both the office work of King's Teens as well as visiting clubs; in fact, she did everything necessary for successfully carrying on this work. This relieved Mike a great deal, although he greatly missed the personal contact with teenagers, for his heart was in young people's work. When possible, he enjoyed speaking at the various club meetings and seeing young people respond to the gospel message.

One day, Mike received a letter from his mother saying his sister, Doris Geer, had written her that she was interested in becoming a Christian. His mother asked if he would go and see Doris. So one night Mike and I drove to Everett, which is about 15 miles from King's Garden, to visit Jack and Doris Geer. They both received the Lord into their hearts that night.

The following Sunday they visited us at the Garden and we went into the dining room to eat, for at that time most of the workers were eating together instead of in their own homes. To my amazement, the man in charge of the dining room that Sunday asked Jack to pray. Knowing what a babe in Christ Jack was, I was really afraid. My fears were unfounded, however, for he offered a very sweet prayer for the food. Jack grew in grace quickly and it was not long before he asked if they might not have a King's Teens Club in their own home. This club was a very successful one and many teenagers were brought to the Lord. When Juanita Berg resigned to be married, Jack received a call from the Lord to take over the King's Teens department. Under his leadership the work has grown tremendously and he is still serving in that capacity.

King's Teens Clubs are held in different homes and there are two counselors for each club. Sometimes the host and hostess in the home serve as the counselors, but the ideal arrangement is to have two counselors in addition to the people in the home. In this way there are enough adults to pray with the teenagers when the need arises. Clubs are held weekly, whichever night of the week is most convenient for each club. At each meeting an opportunity is given for the teenagers to accept Christ as their own personal Savior. Refreshments are served, providing a time of fellowship before they return to their homes.

Sometimes it is very difficult to get a club started in the districts where it is especially needed. Much prayer had been offered for one district. One day a young couple called the King's Teens office. Their home was in this area and they wanted to do something to reach the young people for the Lord. A club was planned and invitations were sent out to the high school teenagers. No young people came the night of the first meeting.

The adults prayed and decided to try again the following week. Again, no one came. The third week, another planned. Seven-thirty in the evening came, and no teenagers. Suddenly voices were heard outside, and out on the sidewalk several teenagers were standing, afraid to come in. They were welcomed into the home and the first club meeting got underway. In this small group there was one pathetic little girl, about 13, very worldly looking, and obviously in need of help. It was for this girl the Lord burdened the hearts of the counselors and they prayed earnestly that she might respond.

The following week there were more teenagers who came, and again this same little girl was there. At the close of that meeting, she gave her heart to the Lord. What a joy it was to see her grow spiritually. Later the Lord showed her she was to become a missionary. She received much opposition at home from her parents, but she remained true to the Lord. All through her school years she maintained a consistent testimony. After graduation from high school she enrolled in Bible school. Now she is preparing to go to the mission field. It is for such young people that King's Teens was started. What a source of satisfaction to those who work in this department, to see young people find God's best for their lives.

Each year in February the King's Teens Valentine's banquet has been held and these banquets have grown both in numbers of teenagers attending and in those who have found Christ as their Savior. An invitation to accept Christ is given at the end of each banquet. The first one was held in the old Seattle Pacific College gymnasium. At that time, there was only the one club meeting in our own home. Many of the teenagers had found the Lord as their Savior and were desirous of doing something to bring their parents under the sound of the gospel. We decided to have a banquet.

Being unlearned in such matters we encountered difficulties. After writing friends in Goldendale, Washington, of our need, we received 16 chickens from which we could make chicken fricassee. What a job that proved to be. I boiled the chickens for some time in a large pan borrowed from the Simpson Bible School and then had the job of taking all the meat from the bones.

Club members and their parents were invited free for this first banquet. Mike was the speaker and since there was no platform of any kind, he stood on a chair to speak. During his talk one of the mothers walked up to him and began to tug at his coat. Mike tried to ignore her but finally he saw she was determined to speak to him. He stopped speaking and leaned down. She told him she wanted to be saved. Being very inexperienced in these matters, Mike was alarmed and exclaimed, "You can't get saved until after I finish speaking." However, she wouldn't wait and finally Mike called to one of the counselors to take her into the other room and counsel with her.

A few years ago a woman came to see Mike in his office. She asked him if he remembered a woman who tugged at his coat and asked to be saved. When he told her he remembered, she said she was the one and assured him she was going on with the Lord. They laughed together over the incident.

The second banquet was held at the Chamber of Commerce building. Each year the banquet grew larger until the room could no longer accommodate all who desired to come. Then it was moved to the Masonic Temple, until that, too, was crowded out. Next the banquet was moved to the armory. In 1961, we knew that even the armory would not be large enough for the numbers indicating they were desirous of coming. It was decided to apply to use an airplane hangar at the Sand Point Naval Air Station.

Permission was miraculously granted, and more than 5,000 teenagers and adults gathered for this event. It was a wonderful sight to see the vast crowd of people sitting in this hangar, most of them young people. The room was decorated with hearts and many flowers, with a large mural at the front depicting the space age. Merv Rosell, the well known evangelist, gave a gripping message. So many young folks poured into the prayer room that the 500 commitment tickets were soon exhausted, as some six or seven hundred young people were dealt with. It was a wonderful sight to see the many who came forward in response to the invitation to accept Christ. I know a great many have accepted the Lord as their Savior at these banquets, for they have contacted us later in large numbers to tell us of their conversion. The banquets have also provided wholesome entertainment for Christian teenagers and a place where they can bring their friends.

Other social events were planned also, to give the teenagers an enjoyable time in a wholesome way. In the fall that we moved to the King's Garden the workers decided to have a large party at Halloween for all the different clubs. Young people came by the hundreds, many of them not members of any club and who had never heard much about Christ before. With several workers able to participate and help, and the tunnels providing the proper Halloween atmosphere, the party was a great success. At the end of the games, before the refreshments were served, a Christian film was shown. An invitation was given to all those at the party to start attending the King's Teens Club nearest their homes.

One year the King's Teens organization made a movie, which was based on a story taken from true life. This film was called "The Teenager" and has been used widely. It has been the means of helping many teenagers realize their need of a Savior. It was a tremendous undertaking to make this film, but it has been a real blessing.

King's Teens also desired to provide a week of Bible camp during the summer for members of the King's Teens Clubs. For a few years, this week was spent at Lake Sammamish Bible Camp. When we moved to King's Garden, the week of camp was held on the grounds. This did not prove too successful, so a camp was rented for two or three summers. Finally a camp on Horse Shoe Lake was leased with an option to buy. Many people began to pray for the money to make the down payment of $21,000 before the option expired. This money was received, the camp was purchased and named King's Teens Miracle Ranch. Truly it came into being on a miracle basis and has been appropriately named.

Now the camping program can be continued all summer long, with several one-week camps. It is a wonderful improvement over anything which King's Teens has had before. Teenagers come for a week of camp life, with much recreation provided—swimming, boating, water skiing, life saving, archery, picnics and games of all kinds—but the main reason for the camp is to give out the gospel story. Many boys and girls have come, who had no interest in spiritual things. They are attracted only by the fun aspect of the camps. They come and they hear how Christ died for them, too, and readily respond to the message. Many Christian young people also have dedicated their lives for His service at these camps. Three-day camps are also arranged during the holiday season between Christmas and New Year's Day. These, too, have been popular with the teenagers. The future for work among teenagers is bright, with great possibilities. The leaders are desirous to have a snow lodge in the mountains so that teenagers might be brought in contact with the gospel through the avenue of skiing.

How often my own heart has been stirred when I have attended some of the camp firesides. The dark night, the glowing fire, and the silhouettes of young people as they have stood and told how the Lord dealt with them, have stamped an indelible image on my mind. I believe a great future is in store for this part of the club ministry, for the blessing of the Lord is resting upon it.

I can look back to the first King's Teens meeting in our home with its four members. (And as Mike has so often said, "There were four teenagers there—two of them were my own children, and they had to come!") The growth and success of King's Teens is an indication of all God can do when He finds someone who is willing to trust Him and act upon His leading.

CHAPTER VI

Among All Nations

"And the gospel must first be published
among all nations."
Mark 13:10

That first fall of 1949 spent at King's Garden was such a busy time and there were many phases of the work clamoring for Mike's attention. However, we knew, too, that we needed to start working with the materials God had already provided. The second ministry, which had been started in a small way before we moved to the Garden, was the printing shop. A small but rather complete press had been given to King's Teens the summer before and had been placed in a rented building. Now it was decided to move the shop to King's Garden for we knew this was one of the ministries God was leading us into. Old Firland had a printing shop in the basement of the Nightingale Building. Our press was installed in the same place theirs had occupied. The two upper floors of the Nightingale Building were used for the Rest Home.

Monroe and Dorothy Johnston and their family moved to the Garden soon after we did. As he was an experienced printer, he took charge of the press. I can remember being amused when Monroe told us he was willing to work half of the day in our farm department, for he knew he did not expect to be busy all day in the printing department. From the day he moved to the grounds, Monroe was more than busy, with many other staff members, often working far beyond the eight hours a day in order to get everything printed. Often when Mike and I returned home from some meeting, we would see the lights on in the print shop and knew that they were working late to provide some printing urgently needed. The printing department has been a most important part of the work and has a varied program.

It did not take long before the space occupied by the press was far too small. They operated in crowded quarters for some years. In 1959, a cement-block building was erected on the grounds for the use of the King's Press. The provision of this spacious, beautiful building made it possible to greatly enlarge this department.

The well equipped shop now includes a Linotype, two platen presses, three offset presses, a photographic department, bindery with power cutter, and a folding machine. It has indeed grown since the day Mrs. Spidell gave King's Teens her small printing shop. Mike visited Mrs. Spidell shortly before she went to be with the Lord and she told him how grateful she was that she had obeyed the Lord and given her shop to be used for Him.

There is also addressograph equipment for the letter service. Many missionaries overseas use the service provided by King's Press for the printing and mailing of their monthly prayer letters. They are enthusiastic in their praise for the beautiful work done on their letters.

Priority is given to the printing needs of the Garden; booklets to advertise the departments and the Garden as a whole; King's Teens materials, such as chorus books and Bible studies; business forms of various kinds;

printing of *The Sceptre* (the school annual); *The King's Herald* (the King's Garden monthly publication); the list is endless of printing needs to be done for the work of King's Garden.

Missionary printing and original publications of gospel literature are produced, many in foreign languages. Many tracts have been printed, and, of these, a large portion have been children's seasonal tracts. Over one million copies of two Halloween tracts alone were printed for one Halloween season. People have found it an excellent way to get the gospel out. On Halloween, children come to the door asking for treats, and along with the treat the hostess gives the children a tract, based on a Halloween story.

For whatever time is available after the above priorities are met, King's Press does some printing for other Christian organizations. How much of this is done depends on how much missionary and Garden printing is needed and also, how large a staff the Press has. A good share of the time, there are not enough people in this department to do all the work which is waiting to be done. Boys and girls who are attending our high school are given the privilege of learning to print if they wish and they work for an hour or two after school, learning all the different aspects of the trade. Many of them serving an apprenticeship in our shop, are able to find work in the printing trade after graduating from high school. Also, candidates for the mission field have been given the opportunity to learn how to print as a part of their training. Several missionaries now on the field are printing in foreign languages because they learned the printing trade at King's Press. Literature for the foreign mission fields is of ever increasing importance as indigenous people are learning to read in large numbers. Helping to train missionaries for this work is one of the valuable aspects of our printing press. As the people of the different lands learn how to read, they are eager to have something to read and it is so important what kind of literature they are given. Good Christian literature is needed to satisfy this hunger of the people.

The work of printing might sound prosaic and uninteresting to some, but the staff who work in the printing department do not feel this way. Perhaps it would be interesting for you to share the testimonies of some of the staff of the King's Press: "To the casual observer, King's Press might seem to be a gloomy place full of bales of paper, noisy machines, and confusion, but to me it might be a mission outpost. As I gather the pages of a gospel tract in a tongue unknown to me, I imagine the eager outstretched hands as the missionary distributes them and I pray that the news may reach them before it is too late. Proofreading a Tagalog song book, letter by letter, is not tedious when one realizes that soon a new brother will be singing, 'Jesus Loves Me,' who only a few months ago had never heard the name of Jesus."

Here is another testimony:

"Books I helped prepare with my own hands have traveled leagues, over ocean and desert, to be caught up by eager hands over there. Gospel portions in their own tongue, which we helped make possible, may be the first literature of any kind received by some newly literate tribe hungry for reading. This is the thrill we know at King's Press. To arm missionaries with gospel literature is as urgent as to send missionaries themselves."

We know that the need for printing is endless to satisfy the world's literacy requirements and that King's Press is a very important cog in supplying the printed materials needed.

To the staff in this department, this ministry is very interesting for they know how vital it is.

CHAPTER VII

The Crown of Glory

"The hoary head is a crown of glory, if it be found in the way of righteousness."
Proverbs 16:31

It had been in August when we moved out to old Firland and began to clean and renovate the place. We expected to hear at any time that the county commissioners had come to a decision about leasing the property to us, but September went by, then October, and still there had been no final word.

On one of Mike's periodic trips down to see the county commissioners, they asked him if he would consider starting an old people's home in connection with our home for teenagers. They advanced two reasons. One was that there was a great need in the Seattle area for homes for elderly people and the other reason was that the income from such a place would be a help to us financially. Mike agreed that it was a worthwhile suggestion and as soon as the administration building was renovated, he started the men on the work of remodeling the Nightingale Building for use as a Rest Home. This he did in spite of the fact that the lease had not yet been signed.

There was a long corridor on each side of this structure, running the full length of it, but only screened in. The rooms opened into these corridors on the two identical floors. We knew it would be necessary to have these corridors glassed in before elderly people would be comfortable there.

A Christian glazier contacted us about installing the glass at a great discount, and it did not take long before the work was all completed. Each room was painted in attractive colors, the floors tiled and new curtains hung at the windows. Everything possible was done to make the Rest Home a place of beauty and peace for those who would be living there.

One evening when the work was completed, I had an errand to run in that direction and I stopped in just at dusk to see the completed renovation. As I stood there gazing at the shining cleanliness, my heart was stirred. God came very close to me in that moment and I will never forget the few seconds I stood there visualizing the restful atmosphere the ones who would live there in the future would enjoy. It was only a fragment of time, then I went on my way, but I will never forget that experience of looking into the future of the Rest Home.

What I visualized that night really came true. The Rest Home has been a blessing not only to those who live there, but to the whole of King's Garden.

Francis and Deirdre Nevan and their little girl were among the workers who came to the Garden that first fall. Francis began to help on the painting crew for there was much to be done in that line. When the Rest Home opened, he was asked to take charge of that department. He was entirely untrained in working with older people for his work had been with young people. I remember his telling me he went over to the Rest Home office, sat down at the desk and prayed, "Lord, what do I do now?" The Lord met his need and it was not long before the Rest Home was a smoothly functioning department.

When the older people began to move in, one by one, we had more opportunity of getting acquainted with them than we did in later years, for there were not as many as now. One morning Mike spoke in the Garden Chapel and when he asked if there were those who would like to accept Christ as their Savior, a man from the Rest Home put up his hand. When Mike talked with him after the meeting, he said he always put up his hand for salvation at every meeting he attended for he wanted to be sure God would accept him. Mike did his best to give him assurance of a complete salvation so that he did not need to accept the Lord over and over again. Because of his age, he had a hard time understanding this. Finally, in desperation, Mike asked him if he would like to receive the same deed to heaven that he had received. He eagerly said he would, so Mike wrote on a piece of paper, Romans 10:13, "For whosoever shall call upon the name of the Lord shall be saved." The man carefully put this in his shirt pocket and whenever Mike would see him he would ask, "Are you saved?"

Mr. A would reach for the paper and read the verse and answer, "Yes." Finally the paper was all worn out but by that time the scripture was in Mr. A's heart and he could quote his salvation verse.

There were other notable conversions among our Rest Home people. One man who came to us was a Mohammedan, and he accepted the Lord one day. It was a great joy to hear him as he walked around the grounds, calling out, "Praise the Lord!" When someone moves into the Rest Home and does not know Christ, the Christians in the home have a great burden to see him saved. They pray much and also speak a word in season. There have been many who have found the Lord as their Savior in the sunset years of their lives.

Many prayer warriors have lived in our Rest Home and much prayer has gone up from that place all day long. They are praying not only for the success of King's Garden, but they are willing and anxious to take any individual prayer requests which come to them. So often when someone is going to be speaking at a meeting, word is sent over to the people in the Rest Home to pray as the message goes out. Small wonder that the many avenues of service have been blessed, for much prayer has gone up to heaven for them.

A chapel meeting is held for the residents every morning. The speakers are varied—missionaries passing through the Garden, other visiting guests, Garden workers—and these meetings are greatly enjoyed by those living there. Speakers often report that they receive a great blessing from speaking at the Rest Home for these people are very attentive and eager to hear.

Everything possible is done to make life enjoyable for those who live in our Rest Home. Some guests have hobbies and these are encouraged to provide hours of pleasure and recreation. Some of the men enjoy working with the flowers and shrubs and they have contributed much to the loveliness of the gardens. The women enjoy needlework and have organized a group known as the King's Daughters, taking their name from the Bible in Psalm 45:13, "The King's daughter is all glorious within: her clothing is of wrought gold." Each Wednesday afternoon these ladies meet to hear a missionary message, to pray for missions, and to discuss ways to forward missionary work. Other afternoons some may be found rolling bandages to be sent to missionaries in the leper colonies. Some are busy at various types of handwork. At the Missionary Conference which is held each year, these ladies have a booth where handwork is sold. Quilts, afghans, rugs, crochet work, aprons, and many other gift items are for sale and all the proceeds go to help missionary work.

A chapter of WCTU (Women's Christian Temperance Union) is organized among the women of the Rest Home and meetings are held regularly.

A party is usually held once a month to honor those who have a birthday during the month. At Christmas time a program is given for them and gifts passed out to each resident. Once a year a picnic is planned at the warmest time of the year for all who are physically able to attend.

Each Friday afternoon one of the school busses is used to take our older friends shopping in the local area. One day, seeing the faces of older people peering through the school bus windows, a pedestrian was heard to murmur, "They must be the alumni."

These are some of the ways the Rest Home staff endeavors to provide change and recreation for those who are living in the home. Some of our high school girls work in the Rest Home for an hour or two a day, and as our older friends have become acquainted with the girls, they have become friends and the older people have had the opportunity for fellowship with young people. Sometimes the girls have confided their problems to the older women and these have been brought to the Lord in prayer.

When any of the Rest Home residents became ill, it was necessary to send them to the hospital in an ambulance. This was cause for much distress among them, for they wanted to remain at King's Garden. After the basement of the Nightingale Building was vacated by the printing department, it was decided to start a small hospital so that the ones who were ill could be cared for and it would not be necessary to send them to the hospital. Sunset Hall was opened in the winter of 1959 and has been a blessing to those who have been ill. As one resident put it, "We want to go to heaven from King's Garden, not from a hospital." Benefits from the Rest Home to King's Garden go far beyond the two reasons given by the county commissioners for opening a Rest Home. It has provided a home for older people, which was greatly needed, and it has been a help to the King's Garden financially. Besides this, however, the prayer life of the residents there has been a great factor in the success of King's Garden. Also, having the older people on the grounds has helped to give a family atmosphere to the young people's work, and we know this department was really raised up by the Lord.

I am getting ahead of my story once more, for the Rest Home was opened the last week in November, 1949, but I must retrace my steps to keep the continuity of my narrative. Let me tell you about the meeting on November 14. We had been patiently waiting to hear that the county commissioners had come to a decision about leasing the property to us. Shortly before November 14, Mike was told of the meeting which was going to be held on that day and that he would be given an opportunity to present his case at that time. He was given no assurance that King's Garden would be leased to us.

Mike asked many people to pray when he went down to this public hearing. Other people were at the meeting also, asking to lease old Firland and many of them offered large sums of money. However, when they were asked what they intended to do with the entire place, none of them had a ready answer. Some wanted to start a Rest Home for older people, but they had no need for more than one or two of the buildings. Mike had done much planning and praying. When it was his turn to make his application, he had a well-laid-out program with a purpose for each building. He also gave them his promise in Jeremiah. When he was through speaking, one commissioner said, "The only one who has mentioned the Lord is Mike Martin, so let us lease old Firland to him for $1 a year. Let's try the Lord's way." This motion was speedily seconded and passed. Many of our friends were present at that meeting and when this motion was passed, they began to praise the Lord. It was a tremendous occasion. Even though the commissioners reminded Mike that this lease was only for five years and that the improvements we were putting in would not be ours at the termination of the lease, but would revert back to the county, Mike told the commissioners repeatedly that he had God's promise. He was going to proceed just the same as though we already owned it.

There were those who were opposed to our receiving this lease and much adverse publicity was given to what we were going to do. An illustration of this happened one night at almost midnight. One of the workers came and woke Mike, saying someone was sitting in his office. After hurriedly dressing, Mike went into his office. A man was sitting at Mike's desk, with his feet on the desk, smoking a big cigar. When Mike asked him what he wanted, he said he was a newspaper reporter who had come out to investigate what we were doing, for he thought we were separating children from their parents. Mike was outraged and said if he was a newspaper reporter, he should have some credentials. The man did not have any and Mike told him very emphatically to get out. The next day Mike called the newspapers in Seattle to ask if they had sent anyone out to investigate us, but they did not know anything about it. We found out later the man lived in the vicinity of King's Garden.

We now had a lease, with three different ministries already underway. There was still much to be done, for we were looking forward to the day when we could start our schools and have dormitories for boys and girls from broken homes. This had been the vision Mike had received from the Lord and this plan was ever before him. Others of our workers caught the vision of this type of work, too, and much prayer and labor went into bringing the schools into existence.

One of Mike's jobs was to secure the materials necessary for all the remodeling work to be done, and one day when he was downtown, he noticed a warehouse with a lot of firtex in it. He asked the manager if he would sell all he had on hand for one-half the current price. Mike looked at the amount of firtex which he could see in the warehouse and estimated about how much it was. He told the owner he would take all that he had at that price. The man refused and said he could not sell for such a cheap price. However, the next day he called and said if Mike would take all the firtex he had, he would agree to this price. Mike was thinking of the amount he had seen in the warehouse and jumped to the conclusion that this was all. He estimated we would need about $1,500 to pay for it. After asking our workers to pray for $1,500 to pay for the firtex when it was delivered, he left on a business trip. When he returned after a few days, our men had hauled in most of the firtex. Only then he found out that actually $7,000 worth of this commodity had been purchased. The man had carloads of firtex which Mike did not see in the warehouse.

You can imagine the thoughts which went through Mike's mind at this development, for he had promised to pay cash when the firtex was all delivered and we did not have this much money. Mike was in a real predicament. The Lord had answered the prayers of the workers and $1,500 had come in through contributions, but now this was not nearly enough to pay the $7,000 which would be due the next day. That noon after our lunch, all of our workers knelt around the table and prayed for the Lord to undertake. By evening $4,000 was on hand. During the evening someone opened the door to our apartment and threw several bills into our hall, without letting us see who it was. The last thing before bedtime that night, a man came to tell us he wanted to give us some money. The amount he said was the exact amount still needed. Needless to say, the King's Garden had firtex piled everywhere.

CHAPTER VIII

Be Gentle Unto All Men

"And the servant of the Lord must not strive;
but be gentle unto all men. . . ."
II Timothy 2:24

Because the King's Garden came into being in such a rush and we were inexperienced, there was no regular procedure for accepting workers. No one received a proper interview. As a result. some workers came who were not called of God, and things happened, some amusing, others tragic. One lady asked if a friend of hers could come to the Garden to work. Soon after she came, we had a fire in the top floor of the administration building near where this girl had her room. The fire started late at night. She reported seeing the smoke, and we all commended her for reporting the fire so promptly. However, when the Fire Marshall came out to investigate, he asked who had reported the fire and asked to speak with the young lady. It was only a short time later that he came back and told us she was the one who had set the fire. She had done this in order to call attention to herself.

Another incident which proved we needed to be more careful in selecting our workers, happened one afternoon when Mike was out of town. I was sitting in the office peacefully typing when I heard a loud commotion in the hall. I hurried out to see what was the matter and saw our cook chasing his helper down the hall with a butcher knife in his hand and shouting, "I am going to kill you." This same cook would only serve soup for lunch and for as long as he was with us we could always depend on having soup for our noon meal. Mike got so desperate he called the cook in and asked him if he would please change his menu for everyone was tired of soup. But his reply was that as long as he was the cook, we would get soup for lunch. I think we were all quite relieved when he left us.

As a result of incidents of this kind, a regular procedure was set up for accepting workers, and we were much more careful to investigate those who wanted to come to work. I had just read in one of Amy Carmichael's books where she had written, "Guard your gates well." I brought the passage to Mike to read and he agreed "our gates" indeed needed guarding.

Other problems developed that first winter. Difficulties with some of our staff brought many trials. Some of the workers began to question Mike's leadership and he went to the Lord about it. He told the Lord he was willing to resign as leader, but before he could resign it would be necessary for a new leader to be raised up, one who could organize the work in the right way. During this time of testing, God gave Mike a scripture which he could bank on, and showed him definitely that he had been chosen for this work. He said Mike should "occupy temporarily" until such time that God, not man, should remove him. This scripture was found in Isaiah 41:9-15:

"*Thou* whom I have taken from the ends of the earth, and called thee from the chief men thereof, and said unto thee, *Thou art* my servant, I have chosen thee and not cast thee away. Fear thou not; for I *am* with thee: be not dismayed; for I *am* thy God: I will strengthen thee; yea, I will help thee; yea, I will uphold thee with the right hand of my righteousness. Behold, all they that were incensed against thee shall be ashamed and confounded: they shall be as nothing; and they that strive with thee shall perish. Thou shalt seek them and shalt not find them, *even* them that contended with thee: they that war against thee shall be as nothing, and as a thing of nought. For I the Lord thy God will hold thy right hand, saying unto thee, Fear not; I will help thee. Fear not, thou worm Jacob, *and* ye men of Israel; I will help thee, saith the Lord and thy redeemer, the Holy One of Israel. Behold I will make thee a new sharp threshing instrument having teeth: thou shalt thresh the mountains, and beat them small, and shalt make the hills as chaff."

From the time Mike received this promise we began to see the ones who questioned his leadership begin to leave, one by one, without anyone saying anything to them. It was a time of purging in our own lives as we saw God begin to move in our behalf. The nucleus of workers who were left, were those who were heart and soul in the work, and God began to send us other workers to take the place of those who left. An interviewing committee was formed to talk to all who applied and they endeavored to ascertain if they were being sent by God. People came who were well-trained in their trades and professions, and in love with the Lord. The work of King's Garden was shaken down to a solid foundation, upon which we could begin to build.

Jim Seibert was a man who was an expert in working with machinery and in engineering. He and his family moved to the Garden and he was of inestimable help in many departments, supervising the boiler construction in the power house, helping to build the radio station, and in many other ways was a tremendous asset. He also served as Assistant Pastor in our chapel.

Ragner Bergren and his family came to us from Montana. No one ever called him any other name than "Rags." He became our first purchasing agent. Later when a need arose for someone to take over the kitchen, Rags volunteered and served in that capacity until the Lord called him home in April, 1951. He was the first worker to pass away while serving at King's Garden. His wife, Maud, was matron in the Rest Home but after Rags' homegoing, she went back to her home in Montana.

It was a source of great comfort to Mike to have the Lord call his own brother, Vernon, and his family to work at the Garden. When we visited Vernon and Doris in Bellingham, we would tell them all about what we were planning to do. After we moved to King's Garden, they came to visit us here and Vernon began to see the great need of workers and gradually the Lord began to speak to them about coming and helping. They saw God work some miracles for them in order that their bills could be all paid so that they would be free to come. Vernon came expecting to work in the tool department, but it did not take long until he became Business Manager. He continued in this work until he became Assistant to the President. Mike often told me how thankful he was that Vernon was working at the Garden because he was so dependable. These and other workers of this caliber began to move into the Garden and the work began to grow.

I knew my own place of service was to help Mike in the office work, but I felt I should do something in addition to the office work in order to show the other staff members I was willing to do physical work too. As I prayed, the Lord showed me that I could get breakfast on Sunday mornings and allow the workers in the kitchen department to sleep in. Not being experienced in cooking for a large group. I was rather at a loss as to how to proceed. Finally I told Mike he should go to a bakery on Saturday afternoon and get some pastry and I would serve that with cold cereal and bananas. It worked very well and I continued to get breakfast on Sunday for some months, serving the same menu each Sunday. This has never been changed and to this day the menu for Sunday breakfast is pastry, cold cereal, and bananas. In the last few years Mike would refer to this experience in a joking way, saying that I might not have left my imprint on much of the schedule of King's Garden, but I had certainly established the menu for Sunday breakfast.

Our working staff has continued to be somewhat fluid. Many people come to us as workers and after being in the missionary atmosphere of this organization and hearing missionary speakers, they receive a call from God to go out as missionaries to the foreign field, or to other Christian service at home. Though we miss them greatly, we do not hinder them in any way from going. Rather, we do all we can to help them raise their support and supply their outfits for their new service. What did grieve Mike much was to see someone start in Christian service and then draw back because the cost was more than they wished to pay. They looked back to the "leeks and garlic of Egypt" and left again to take secular work where they would make good salaries.

CHAPTER IX

Blessed Be the Lord

*"Blessed be the Lord, who daily loadeth us
with benefits. . ."*
Psalm 68:19

As we looked forward to the time when we could open our schools, we knew we had many needs in regard to this new undertaking. Mike had been told of commodities which the government made available for schools and he was given the name of the government agent he was to see, to receive approval for securing materials for our schools. As Mike was praying on the morning before his appointment with Mr. B., he felt strongly that God told him to give the man his testimony. This was not in accordance with Mike's reasoning at all, for he was fearful that if he began his appointment by testifying to Mr. B., he would not get his approval.

However, by the time Mike reached Mr. B.'s office, he knew if he was to obey the Lord, he would have to testify before stating his mission. As Mike began to give his testimony, this government agent grew very interested. Finally he walked over to his door and locked it, so that they would not be interrupted. For over an hour Mike told of what the Lord had done in his life and when he had finished, this man said, "I do not have the peace which I can see you have. I long to have it, but . . . I cannot believe as you do. But you surely did not come in just to tell me these things. What can I do for you?" Mike then told him of the approval it was necessary to obtain to receive free commodities, and immediately the authorization was given. Eventually Mike was able to lead this man to receive the Lord Jesus Christ and they became good friends. Mike also went to the office of the Seattle public schools and asked them to let us have anything they were planning to throw away. Through this department, King's Garden received many truckloads of things which we could use. Mike then discovered that the head of the educational department in Olympia was a boyhood friend of his and through his help we began to get war surplus materials.

Firland Sanatorium, now in its new location, was very cooperative, too, donating equipment they no longer needed. One thing they gave us was a fire engine, and our men began to hold fire drills on Saturday mornings to be prepared if more fires occurred. More fires did occur, and one was especially spectacular. We were building a duplex for needed housing and it was almost completed. To dry out the inside of the house, a fire was started in a stove, banked and left for the night. Early in the evening a neighbor near the Garden turned in a fire alarm, and the neighborhood fire department, arriving ahead of our own, found part of the roof going up in a sheet of flame. The fire was quickly extinguished, but a thousand dollars worth of damage had been done.

It was indeed in various ways that God supplied our needs, for we were in need of many things. It was wonderful to see the friendliness of so many people and to realize they wanted to help King's Garden succeed. We were given certain foods in quantities, such as string beans and corn. We endeavored to save these foods by canning them after our work day was over. I can well remember working until midnight some evenings, cutting up string beans and cutting corn off the cobs. However, the canning process must have been faulty; for after a few days, the cans began to explode. We gave up this kind of work, for it was too much to expect the workers to put in such long hours after their regular day's work ended. However, we took one truckload of string beans to a cannery and had them canned and that first winter string beans were almost constantly on the menu.

From the very beginning people gave us used clothing and furniture. It was all such a help. Since none of us received a salary, it was hard for us to have our clothing needs met on the small allowance we received. Often there was not enough money to pay the full allowances, and one half of the allowances was given out. A few times, no money was available to give to the workers. So the clothing which came in was carefully handled and hung on hangers in one of the rooms. A lady was put in charge of giving out the various articles according to the need and sizes. The workers jokingly named this store "The Royal Outfitters." For some years most of my own clothing came through this source. Mike, too, found suits which he could wear and a friend of his, Fred Rady, supplied him with shoes. In over 15 years, I don't believe Mike had more than two or three new pairs of shoes.

When we had been at the King's Garden for ten years, we had an anniversary meeting in a downtown auditorium. Mike happened to tell the newspaper man about his never having new shoes, at the time he was giving him the publicity for the anniversary meeting. We were surprised later to find the following reference had crept into the newspaper account:

"Mike Martin presides over a multimillion-dollar Christian cause, but in ten years he has not been able to afford a new pair of shoes. Martin's shoes, like most of his other clothing, are somebody's castoffs. He owns neither automobile nor home and has no bank balance. Yet Martin will rejoice in the richness of his Christian faith as he presides over King's Garden's tenth anniversary celebration in the Masonic Temple."

Yet it would be misleading not to add that Mike was always well dressed and drove good cars which were supplied by a car dealer in return for radio advertising.

The workers did not require all of the clothing which came in. In August of 1950, there was a severe hurricane in Jamaica and since one of our Rest Home guests had been a missionary there, he was quite concerned. Mr. Axel Fredeen helped Mr. Jesperson crate clothing appropriate to a warm climate and get it ready for shipment. A shipping company volunteered to send this material free of charge to relieve the plight of the Jamaicans.

A short time later this letter was sent to Mr. Fredeen

Dear Mr. Fredeen:

I write to thank you most sincerely for the gift of clothing which you have been good enough to make for the relief of those who suffered in the August hurricane. We are most grateful to Mr.

Jesperson and to you and to all those who assisted in making this gift which is greatly appreciated.
Yours sincerely,
Hugh Foot
Governor of Jamaica.

The furniture which was given to the Garden was used both in the workers' apartments and in and around King's Garden. Tables, chairs, and desks were needed in the offices, and practically everything which came in filled a real need. After a few years an economy store was started on Aurora Avenue, and the extra articles which came in were sold. The money was used to help pay the workers' allowances. In this way it was hoped that they would be able to afford to get a few new things. This store burned down after a few years, and was not been rebuilt at that location. The beautiful new KG Economy Store continues to be of real help to the finances of the Garden.

We realized, too, that when sickness or accidents came, the workers would not be able to pay doctor bills. A small insurance plan was started. We called it our "Emergency Fund" and each worker would pay a certain amount into this fund. This plan proved to be so successful that it still continues today.

Old Firland had names for all the buildings, but now we realized new names were needed for at least part of them, so a committee was formed to consider the matter and bring new names to the workers for approval. Listed are the names of the buildings Firland had and the new names as recommended by the committee, and accepted by the workers :

Firland Names	*King's Garden Names*
Detwiler Building	King's Garden High School
Josef House	King's Garden Grade School
Nightingale Building	The Nightingale Building
Koch Building	Central Hall
Vom Piquet	Nightingale Annex
Pasteur Ward	Sylvan Hall
Isolation Ward I	Girls' Dormitory
Isolation Ward II	Apartments
Administration Building	Administration Building

Mike realized, too, since the work of King's Garden had mushroomed so fast, it was necessary to get it organized on a more firm basis. A committee was formed for each department, to help the head of that department run the work. Many of the men assigned to take charge of a department were inexperienced and needed guidance. Mike was given the scripture in Proverbs 11:14, "Where no counsel is, the people fall; but in the multitude of counselors there is safety." He felt this was God guiding him to surround the leaders with a committee to counsel them.

The workers also met together once a month the first few years, to discuss any problems which they had and to hear reports from each department. However, after the work had grown to large proportions and there were many workers, it was much harder to bring them all together and the workers' business meetings were only held once or twice a year.

One of the departments that was opened after the Rest Home was underway was the laundry. This is part of the work which goes on year after year without much attention being focused on it, but it is a very necessary part of the Garden. Laundry for the Rest Home and for the boys' and girls' dormitories is processed in the same place where Firland had their laundry, on the top floor of the power house.

Many of our people did not have cars and we felt it necessary to have a church service on the grounds for those who desired a local meeting place. Many visitors came to the King's Garden from some distance away and enjoyed attending church on the ground. So we organized the King's Garden Chapel. The Chapel then extended a call to Rev. Alan Inglis to serve as chaplain. He accepted the call and he and his family moved to the Garden in January of 1951.

Everyone loved him and he was "Pastor Al" to the entire Garden. Vannie Inglis served as Supervisor of Women for a number of years.

We encouraged our workers to go to the church of their choice and to remain with whatever denomination they were affiliated with. We did not wish to compete with other churches, but rather to be a help to them. Therefore those who had transportation went to other churches and there were comparatively few workers at the Garden services, yet the chapel was well filled. There were families living near the Garden who attended regularly and a number of our workers who made the Garden Chapel their church home. We also required that the boys and girls in our dormitories attend church at the Garden on Sunday evenings. Mike felt that we should attend church at the Garden, for it gave him a good opportunity to meet many of the visitors. Consideration has been given at various times to building a non-denominational church off the grounds, but the way has been checked thus far.

The King's Garden, Incorporated Board began to meet regularly once a month at the Garden. Some of the board members resigned and others were added to take their places. It was a great responsibility for these seven men, for there were many problems to solve, and at each meeting the members would kneel and each one would pray for wisdom and guidance as they discussed the various matters brought to their attention.

Mike was inexperienced in guiding such a large institution, but though he made mistakes, God was very close to him. He was able to receive from the Lord the leading and help which he so greatly needed.

One day the Lord revealed to him that he should report for duty each day to his heavenly Master. He reminded him that when he worked for the Richfield Oil Company the most important appointment he had was with his district manager. Now that Mike was working for the Lord, the most important appointment of the day was with Him. God told him that he should spend one hour each morning receiving orders from Him. Mike was led to choose the hour between 9:00 and 10:00 A.M., and for years he set this time aside to be alone with the Lord. It took something very important for him to break this rule. I went to work at nine in the morning so the house was empty and quiet as he met the Lord in this way. During this time the Lord gave him very explicit instructions and it was in this way Mike was given the wisdom he needed for the immense task of running King's Garden.

CHAPTER X

The Fear of the Lord

"The fear of the Lord is the beginning of wisdom. . ."
Proverbs 9:10

In the spring of 1950, the staff bent all their efforts towards starting the schools that fall. The main hospital building had been chosen as the home of our high school and the children's hospital as the grade school. In order for these two buildings to be adequate to be used for school purposes, it was necessary to tear out some walls, put in other walls, and make doorways by cutting through cement walls. Many other hard, heavy labors made the days far too short for all that needed to be done. The women were conscripted to help paint as the different carpenter jobs were completed.

As fall approached, we still did not have our school staff. No work had been done on setting up the curriculum nor on all the other tasks necessary in starting a school. Much discussion went on about whether we should endeavor to start or wait for another year. However, the Lord seemed to indicate that we should make the attempt, so the hard work and planning continued. It was decided that tuition would be charged according to the ability to pay. We knew boys and girls from broken homes would have little or no money either for tuition or for room and board. However, we felt people who could afford to should help in the expense of their children's education.

One week before school was to open I was sitting in the office typing, when a well-dressed man came in and asked if we needed teachers, mentioning his field was mathematics. I could see he was just the caliber of man we needed and I immediately called Mike to meet him. We soon found out that Mr. Harold Hemry was our principal, for he was qualified for this office. A few teachers had indicated that if our school actually opened, they would be interested in teaching but it was a tremendous job for the principal to get everything lined up for starting school in such a short time.

We had also received some applications from boys and girls desirous of attending our school, and two or three letters came from teenagers from broken homes, asking if they could come and live with us. One letter came from a 15 year old girl who was living in eastern Washington. Mike went over to investigate the case and he found indeed that Connie was in need of a home; a place of refuge. She was given into Mike's custody and for four years Connie lived at King's Garden, attending high school. She was a perfect example of the teenagers we had been called to minister to. She worked for an hour or two in the Rest Home daily during the week days, and during vacations she would put in a regular shift as a nurse's aid. The older people learned to love her very much for Connie was always kind to them.

When she graduated from high school she came to Mike one day and thanked him for all that had been done for her at King's Garden. Mike told me he could not have received any greater joy than to hear the gratitude of someone who had been helped. After graduation she went on to college and became a practical nurse. She married and moved away, but I know wherever she is today, she is serving the Lord Jesus for she loved Him very much.

Another teenager, a boy named Joe wrote and told us of his need for a home, and he too was in our school through his high school years. We took in several of these teenagers, boys and girls who through no fault of their own, needed a place to live and attend school. They needed a home and love.

As news of our school opening reached Alaska, many Indian boys and girls inquired about attending our school for there were no high schools in Alaska. That first year we had several Indian teenagers with us. One boy especially stands out in my mind, for he was very rough and tough. One day when the boys were playing football he was struck in the face and lost some of his teeth. Sitting there on the ground, spitting out teeth, his comment was, "Now we are having some fun."

Some missionaries serving on the foreign field where there were no high school facilities sent their children to us, and these too lived in our dormitories. There were also many boys and girls living in the north end of Seattle who desired to receive a Christian education and these attended as day students. And, of course, there were the children of our workers.

Almost the very day school opened, Mr. Dutton Hackett offered to be our grade school principal. He and his family moved to King's Garden and we enjoyed their fellowship a great deal. Mr. Hackett loved children and he was always willing to help any of them in any way he could. He knew his heart was weak but he always did more than his share in making our grade school a real success. His stay with us was very brief for in May of 1951 he suffered a heart attack and went to be with the Lord in just a few minutes. We missed him and his family a great deal. A memorial fund was started and the gymnasium which is in the boys' dorm is a memorial to Mr. Hackett and is called "The Dutton Hackett Memorial Gymnasium."

During the summer months, our men had been busy making desks for the grade school for they could be made for less money than buying them. A few chairs with the large arm rest were purchased for the high school.

Mr. Royal Brougham, of the Seattle Post Intelligencer, and Mr. J. W. Langlie, who owned a sporting goods store, were very generous in providing equipment for our school—soft balls, bats, footballs, basketballs, and football and baseball uniforms. This equipment was very useful in providing recreation and physical education for the boys and girls, not only for the schools, but also for the ones who were living in our dormitories.

When the long awaited day came that our schools opened, there were 63 students enrolled in the high school and 63 in the grade school. The freshman class constituted the largest class in the high school, with the eighth and tenth grades a close second. There were seven in the senior class; our oldest boy being one of the seven.

We still did not have any typewriters for the commercial department. A typing class was started without typewriters. The teacher placed a chart on the wall and asked the class to pretend to have typewriters and just strike the table in front of them as they watched the chart. When Mike walked through the school one morning and saw the youngsters doing this, he was downcast, for he could see the great need. The teacher told him there were 15 students in the class, all eager to learn to type. About two weeks went by, and Mike was praying fervently for typewriters. One day we were able to obtain typewriters—brand new Remingtons—through the school department in Seattle. How many typewriters came? Fifteen of course, for God knew how many students were in the class.

Immediately after school opened, the students started a school newspaper. It was interesting to see the initiative they displayed even to the extent of getting advertisements from businesses in the area, to help defray the cost of publishing it. There was a good school spirit from the very first, even though many things were lacking. Most of our first students were real pioneers and worked with a will to make King's High a school with high standards, both scholastically and spiritually. It was decided to publish a school annual the first year and the name chosen for it was "The Sceptre." The inspiration for this name came from the gothic architecture of the buildings, for it reminded the students of knights and clanking armour.

Great emphasis was placed on both music and art in the schools. The Lord signally blessed in both these fields and sent us teachers who were very qualified. A choir and band were soon organized and it was not long before choir robes were supplied. The need for band uniforms was met when the music director saw an ad in a paper in California, that band uniforms were for sale secondhand. He was able to obtain these uniforms for only $100.

For the school theme song the music director wanted a militant Christian song to the old Welch martial music of "Men of Harlech." Ruth Mills, a Garden worker, composed the following lines with a medieval flavor and a note of triumphant faith:

> Youth of King's High, hear Christ call you;
> Let not sin's rough fetters gall you;
> Break the bands that would enthrall you
> Through Christ's mighty name.
> Fell the proud aggressor!
> Claim the land at God's command—
> Your land of promise, God shall bless her!
> While love flies His banner o'er us,
> And while our eyes behold Him glorious,
> Shout that conquering name!

Instead of having the annual sneak day for our graduating class in the spring, as public schools do, our school instituted a retreat for the senior class. Each spring they leave the school for a two day outing, and these times are days of spiritual refreshing and fellowship for the seniors. Many spiritual victories have been won at these retreats making them very worthwhile. One of the little tokens of God's blessing on our schools which especially appealed to Mike was that there were 7 graduating seniors the first year, 14 the second year, 21 the third year and 28 the fourth year. Since seven is God's number, Mike felt that this multiple of seven each year was a special little message to him from God.

Each year our student body grew until the time when there was not room for it to grow any more. The administration of the schools then began to be more selective in their choice of students. They admitted only those whom they felt were students desiring a Christian education and willing to abide by the rules. It is almost impossible to help students who are rebellious and desire their own way; who are not interested in Christian activities.

At the very beginning of our dormitories we endeavored to accept both the Christian boys and girls and those who had been in trouble with the law or who were just unruly and did not desire to obey the rules. We found it was not possible to successfully combine the two types of teenagers.

Because many requests came from parents desiring help for their boys and girls who had gone astray, we began to pray for a school where these needy teenagers could be helped. One day while on a trip to Vancouver, Washington, Mike heard of a school which was going to be vacated when school was out in June, 1956. The Burton Homes School had originally been built in a war-time housing project and had been used by the Vancouver school district for ten years. This school building was 459 feet long, with a gymnasium auditorium, was fully equipped and built on 12 acres of land. We made application to the government to obtain this school for a price, but through an error we applied to the wrong governmental department. This caused much time to elapse while we re-applied and it was nearing time for school to be out in June. This property would then be vacated, leaving the building to the mercy of "hoodlums" and it would not be long before vandalism would make the school unfit for use.

Mike endeavored to secure permission from the government to go in and protect the property, but he was unable to receive an official permission. He went to the superintendent of the school district, who had the keys. Mike told the superintendent, "The Lord is going to give us the school in answer to prayer, and you should give us the keys so that we can protect the site." He looked startled for a moment, then said, "I believe the Lord is going to give you this school," and handed over the keys.

For four months King's Garden had no official permission to occupy the Burton Homes School. We placed a family to live there to guard the property and they began to clean and get it ready to take in boys. During the month of November, 1956, we were given a quit-claim deed free of charge. This was an outright gift, the only stipulation being that it must be used for a school for 20 years. Our offer of several thousand dollars was rejected by one governmental department so that it could be provided free by another department. This was another miracle.

In this school we have been able to care for boys who have been in trouble with the law and other boys who are maladjusted in some way, or emotionally disturbed. Many of these boys have been rehabilitated and become worthwhile citizens. Many, too, have come to know the Lord Jesus Christ as their Savior. Because some of the boys who came to us could not even read, it was necessary to have our own school for them and to give them remedial help. Half of the building is used for school purposes and half has been remodeled for dormitories for the boys. With the gymnasium there for the boys to use and with enough land so that they can have pets and animals in abundance, it has proved to be just the right place for such a project. About 40 or 50 boys are now cared for at one time, but plans for the future call for an expanded program for boys of this type.

In 1961 an organization called Buoyville, in eastern Washington, gave a farm near Mabton, Washington, to King's Garden, to be used as a home for boys. Cash in the amount of $100,000 was also given with the stipulation that it be used for erecting buildings on the farm. When these buildings have been completed many more boys can be received and given a home.

Because there were so many applications from parents and others desiring help for girls of the unruly type, we began to pray for a place to take in girls. A government radio installation was vacated in Astoria, Oregon, and King's Garden made application to receive it in the same way as the Burton Homes School had been given the year before. In November, 1956, a quit-claim deed was signed, giving the property free, with the stipulation that it must be used for school purposes.

So this girls' school was opened, but did not prosper in the same way as the Vancouver Boys' Academy did. We found that working with girls of this type was more difficult than working with boys. They did not respond to the gospel as readily. Perhaps we had not found God's perfect will, but whatever the reason this school did not do well. After a few years it was closed. We have not lost the vision of helping these girls, but we have come to realize that there must be especially trained personnel to run such a boarding school.

After our Christian schools were underway, we began to hear of other Christian schools springing up in the northwest area. We desired to have some means of fellowship with them and felt we could be an encouragement to each other. So the Northwest Fellowship of Christian Schools was formed. There are two divisions to this group. The leaders and administrators of the schools meet together once a year in the fall to discuss their problems and endeavor to help each other. In the spring a musicale is held, with all the different schools participating. The choirs, solos, quartets, and those who play musical instruments sing and play separately and are adjudicated.

On the last evening of the conference, all of the choirs from the different schools sing together as a massed choir. The bands from the schools are also combined and play some numbers. This evening of music is the highlight of the conference. It has been a wonderful opportunity for the students of the different schools to get acquainted and I am sure, too, that the fellowship among the leaders of these schools has also been a help. Thus the vision Mike had of helping boys and girls from broken homes came to fruition in King's High School, The Vancouver Boys Academy, and Buoyville. Boys and girls from normal homes can also be provided a Christian education. We feel that only the surface of the need has been touched and that there is more ahead.

CHAPTER XI

I Am the Lord

" . . For I am the Lord that healeth thee."
Exodus 15:26

There were many times of testing when God led us through some deep waters. We saw many miracles, too. One day I noticed my youngest son was not feeling well and that one side of his face was swollen. He told me he had been struck in the face, so I just thought it was swollen from the blow. However, as it continued to swell and his temperature began to rise, I called our registered nurse from the Rest Home to see him. She called the doctor and then started giving him penicillin. She even came over at midnight to give him another shot, but in the morning she could see he was not getting any better. His fever was high and going higher, until he became delirious.

The King's Garden Board was meeting that day, and they usually met in our front room. When they arrived I told them of Michael's plight and asked if they would come in and pray for him before they started their meeting. They stood by his bedside, and prayed just a simple prayer, and went on into the other room. After they left I stood there alone. I pleaded with the Lord to hear our prayers, bring down the fever, and take away the delirium. As I watched, I was fascinated to see the swelling begin to recede and Michael begin to relax. I waited half an hour and then slipped the thermometer into his mouth. The fever was almost gone. I waited another 15 minutes and again I took his temperature. This time it was completely normal.

I was overjoyed and called the nurse. She came over to see him and told me how concerned she had been for if the infection had reached his brain, he would not have lived. She told me she realized how ill he had been, but was afraid to let me know. Instead, she had gathered the nurses together and they had prayed for our boy.

Another time of testing was when Mike went on a business trip to the Yakima Valley and while he was there he began to feel very weak. Finally he decided it was necessary to secure medical help. After an examination the doctor told Mike that he was taking him immediately to the hospital; that he was bleeding internally and that he already had lost 53% of his blood. If he did not immediately receive blood transfusions his veins would collapse and he would die. I received a phone call telling me of his illness and in the evening our chaplain drove me to Yakima to be with Mike. He began to respond to treatment and after about ten days he was able to return home. While we were gone, the boilers for heating our buildings gave up entirely; and as it was winter time and cold, this worked a real hardship on all the residents of King's Garden. It was necessary to secure new boilers immediately which put a severe strain on our finances.

This problem cast Mike on the Lord as never before, for he was powerless to do anything about the situation. God used this experience to show Mike that the work was not dependent upon him alone. It was His work and He could care for it even though Mike was ill.

After we returned to Seattle Mike was still very weak. One afternoon he began to have a temperature which alarmed me. I could see his heart beating in the pulse of his throat and I knew he was getting quite ill. One of his friends came in that afternoon to visit Mike and when he saw how ill he was, he laid his hand on Mike's head and began to pray, partly in Norwegian. I was standing by the bed and did not close my eyes, but continued to watch Mike as the prayer went on. Even as I watched, the pulse began to subside and I knew the temperature was going down. When the prayer ended I slipped a thermometer into Mike's mouth and the reading was normal once more.

From that time on Mike had periodic times of internal bleeding and was in the hospital once or twice each year. The doctors could not ascertain what was wrong, although an ulcer was suspected. Finally Mike went through a well known clinic in Seattle and the verdict they gave us was that there was no ulcer but that he had a blood vessel in his stomach which was too near the surface and when Mike would eat something which was a little rough, the blood vessel would break open. He was told to stay away from food with seeds such as raspberries, and nuts. His health had never been robust since the time of his first heart attack and it was necessary for him to claim the strength he needed from day to day. I longed to give him of my own splendid health and strength, but of course that was not possible. All I could do was to help him in any way I could and try to curb his tremendous ambition to accomplish all he could for the Lord. I felt he could accomplish just as much if he did not drive himself to exhaustion until he would be ill again. However, his joy in serving the Lord was so great, it was hard for him to hold back. Also I was a little afraid to say too much because I know he had a call of God upon him and I did not want to frustrate God's plans, so the most I felt I could do was to keep cautioning him about overworking and to urge him to take time for his naps.

He also suffered from reoccurring attacks of laryngitis whenever he caught cold. He would lose his voice and would go around whispering to people. It was rather amusing to me to hear many of the people who talked to him during these times, begin to whisper too. He would whisper to them and they would forget and whisper to him in return. However, this ailment was a real trial to him for often when he would have a speaking engagement lined up, his voice would leave him. It would be necessary then to send a substitute to take his place.

Living in the administration building had its disadvantages, for we were eating in the dining room. Those who desired information from Mike would come and sit with us while we ate. This kept Mike from having a time of relaxation while he ate his meals. Also people would knock on the door of our apartment a great many times a day and far into the night. We decided that it would be necessary for us to move into another apartment and to cook our own meals. We moved into the small apartment which was over the school store on the grounds. Even though it was upstairs and necessitated climbing stairs several times a day, it was a great improvement over the other apartment. We lived in this place for about seven years and enjoyed the quietness of it very much.

One of Mike's endearing characteristics was his great love for people and concern to see them find the Lord. As he grew acquainted with men in business through the work of King's Garden he would have a great burden to have them come to know the Lord. Several of these men can call him their spiritual father.

One day, Dean McLean, who was then one of the county commissioners, came out to see the King's Garden. He was walking around the grounds rather dejected, when Mike spied him and walked out to talk with him. Seeing that he was troubled, Mike asked him to come into his office. There he proceeded to testify to Mr. McLean telling him how he found the Lord Jesus Christ and the peace and joy which this had brought him. It did not take long until Mr. McLean fell to his knees and began to pray for God's forgiveness. Then he began to sing in a beautiful tenor voice one of the old hymns. This was the start of a great friendship between these two men. I have a little devotional book which he gave Mike, in which Mr. McLean has written, "I love you, cause you brought me back." A few years later, Mr. McLean went to be with the Lord.

This man was one of many who found the Lord in Mike's office. The last few years of Mike's life he became known through his radio messages, and people would come to him seeking help. He was never too weary or burdened with the cares of his work, to be concerned with those who needed help. There were several times when he was called late at night after we were asleep and someone would be on the phone, asking if Mike would come to his office and pray with them. As the years went on, Mike learned that when he became too weary with the burden of the work, that he should get away for a rest. We would slip away for a day or two. Sometimes we would go to Garland Mineral Springs, to the ocean, or often we would just rent a motel near Seattle. These times would be periods of complete relaxation for him and he would spend most of the time in bed, just reading and resting. We would spend part of the time in praying over the various problems facing him at the moment, and in just talking together about what was best to do. He often told me it was a great help to him in just talking to me about problems. As he talked, rather just thinking aloud, his mind would be clear as to what he was to do. Then completely rested and relaxed we would return to the King's Garden and take up the reins once more.

However, since Mike saw that he needed to get away for rest and relaxation, he could see the need for our workers to get away also. He began to pray for a place where, when they had time off from work, they could slip away, and get away from the pressure which surrounded them at the Garden. Finally a place in Cannon

Beach, Oregon, was made available for lease with an option to buy. This beautiful spot was right on the ocean and very near the Cannon Beach Bible Camp. There were 11 cabins on the grounds and also a good sized lodge. It was an old landmark of the early days of Oregon history when stage coaches used the lodge as a stopover place in their travels. This place was renamed Grace Haven. A caretaker was placed in charge of it. The cabins were rented during the summer months and the lodge was in great demand by church groups on weekends all the year around. Though this was a wonderful place, the distance from the Garden made it prohibitive for many of our workers to take advantage of the restful atmosphere. We had hoped that the rental of the cabins and the lodge would allow the Garden to break even on the finances. This did not prove to be the case. The cost of keeping staff at Grace Haven all the year around was high and it was a continual financial drain for the King's Garden. Even though it was a Christian ministry which was very worthwhile, after a few years the decision was made to relinquish Grace Haven. However, it was taken over by another Christian group and the ministry of Grace Haven is being continued.

CHAPTER XII

My Thoughts Are Not Your Thoughts

"For My thoughts are not your thoughts, neither are your ways My ways, saith the Lord."
Isaiah 55:8

As the time approached for our five year lease to expire, we became concerned about what would happen next. The county commissioners were very sympathetic to our work and wanted to help us. They could not sell old Firland to us direct without a public auction, and only if the Tuberculosis Association decreed they no longer desired to make use of old Firland. They suggested that a bill be placed through the House of Representatives and the Senate. The bill, called House Bill 191, was introduced and passed unanimously in the House of Representatives. This provided that the county commissioners of class A counties could dispose of tuberculosis property without competitive bid when the property was no longer needed for tuberculosis purposes.

When the bill was sent to the senate it did not receive the same enthusiastic support and was "pigeon-holed" which meant that it was tabled, and the senators did not intend to bring it to a motion.

This information about the bill was passed on to Mike by one of his friends. He decided that the two of us should go to the capitol in Olympia and stay there for a week. He wanted to see what he could accomplish by lobbying on the senate floor. We stayed in a motel at night and each day we would spend in the Senate. I was very interested, sitting on the side lines, to see how the Senate operated. It was the first time I had seen our government in action. Mike went on the senate floor, talking with various senators and endeavoring to get the bill out of its "pigeon-hole" so that it could be voted on. He made progress day by day, but he did not have enough time to accomplish his purpose. The bill was not brought out until the evening when the Senate would adjourn. When midnight came, the Senate closed, and Bill 191 was the next one to be voted on. This seemingly was a defeat from a worldly standpoint, but we were not disheartened and realized we evidently had not found God's will in the matter.

Mike therefore began negotiations for having our lease renewed for the longest period of time possible. There was much opposition from many groups who did not want us to continue to lease Firland. Mike asked for a 35 year lease, but after much deliberation, we were given a 10 year lease for $1 a year. Mike still had assurance that the promise "I will give the city" meant that King's Garden would be owned and would not continue to be on a lease basis, but he was just waiting for God's timing.

Each year we had had a dinner and invited the county commissioners and other officials to come out and see what was being accomplished at King's Garden. These were always enjoyable affairs. It was a pleasure to be able to entertain these guests and express our appreciation to them in this way. After our lease was renewed, we again invited them to come to a dinner in

May of 1954, to show our appreciation for their kindness to us. The Garden seemed especially lovely that spring, with the various flowering trees in bloom, and we did our best to provide a nice dinner.

Arthur B. Langlie, who was then Governor of the state of Washington, was invited to this dinner. There were testimonies from some of our high school students, especially from those who were from broken homes, telling of how they had been helped. Two of our Rest Home residents gave a brief talk about what King's Garden had meant to them. Our high school band played and our choir sang. Then Governor Langlie spoke. "As Governor of the state of Washington," he said, "I am very proud that we have people who have faith as you do and the love of Christ, and are willing to give some of that love back to others who need it."

When called on for comments, the chairman of the county commissioners expressed the conviction that the lease to King's Garden of the former Firland property was one of the finest deals they had made since they had become commissioners.

Later on, because of our long struggle to meet the housing needs of our workers, the maintenance crew began to think and plan how to meet this need. Two duplex dwellings were built on the grounds, but this was only a small portion of the housing needed. Mike began to think and pray about how to secure more homes for workers. He was able to secure six houses from the Seattle Housing Authority, but it was necessary to move the houses from where they were situated.

He went to the county commissioners to ask permission to put the houses on the tract of land adjacent to the Garden of Prayer. He promised the houses would be made presentable, adding with a smile, "It is all right with the Lord."

The chairman of the county commissioners replied, "If it's all right with Him, it's certainly all right with this board." These six dwellings were a big help in meeting the need at that time. However, all through the years it has been a continuous struggle to secure more and more places for workers to live, for the staff has continued to increase. A motel near the grounds was purchased on payments, which provided some housing, and for the last few years it has been necessary to rent houses off the grounds in order to provide homes for all the families.

CHAPTER XIII

Go Ye Into All the World

"Go ye into all the world and preach the gospel to every creature."
Mark 16:15

From its inception, King's Garden was very missionary minded. In fact, even before there was a King's Garden, our high school clubs were concerned with missionary needs. One couple who were counselors in the club which met in our home went to Germany as missionaries. They wrote back to us of the need for clothing and food which they saw while ministering to the people in their area. Our club began to gather clothing and food and sent several boxes overseas. The family who was in charge of the King's Teens work in the Yakima Valley went to Japan as missionaries. This all helped to focus our eyes on the mission field. When a man who had been a frequent speaker in our clubs told us he and his family were going to China, the club members decided they would help to support their little girl. Each month part of the offerings of the clubs was sent to help in her support.

Impetus was given to starting a missions department at King's Garden when a family came to us from Australia. Mr. and Mrs. Lyall Lush and their three children came to King's Garden, saying they had been called of God to come to King's Garden as missionaries. Mr. Lush became the head of our missions department and did much to help us to further the cause of missions. Our slogan became, "A Missionary to the Missionaries." We did all we could to help.

Missionaries could come to King's Garden and stay as our guests for two weeks before leaving for the field and also upon their return for furlough. While they were with us, the missions department would do all they could to line up speaking engagements for those desiring to do deputation work. We could provide help with purchasing supplies for them wholesale, printing their prayer letters, and helping with their packing. When time came for them to leave by plane or boat, one of the workers would provide transportation for them and see that their supplies were placed on the dock for shipment. It was a joy to have so many missionaries passing through the Garden, giving us the opportunity to meet them and have fellowship with them.

Our first missionary rally was held in February, 1955. Because of the crowds of people who attended, our high school auditorium was far too small. We knew we would need more space, both for the meetings and for the display booths of the various mission societies.

The next year a tent was rented and erected on the grounds. The booths from the various missionary societies were set up in the gymnasium in the boys' dormitory. Because it was cold weather, the men piped steam into the tent which made it fairly comfortable. These conferences have been held each year since and have grown both in numbers who attend and also in pledges of money to help in missionary work. Missionaries come from all over the world to be there and enjoy being with others of like mind. They are also given an opportunity to tell of their work and what some of their needs are. Especially interesting has been the session for the women. As women missionaries have told of their lives on the field, mentioning the hardships they have been called to go through, hearts have been greatly stirred.

At these conferences people have found the Lord as their Savior; others have been called to the mission field as a result of attending the meetings. Many interesting incidents have happened. One evening one of our workers was singing a solo in the tent. As his beautiful baritone soared out, a man walking along the road near the Garden heard the song. He came to stand in the doorway of the tent, listening intently. After the song ended he sought out a missionary standing near the door, asking him to help him find Christ.

It began to be the usual procedure that after the conference ended to have some of our own workers tell us that they had received a call to the mission field. About 75 of our former workers are now serving the Lord in various parts of the world. In addition to this, thousands of dollars have been pledged to help in the support of missionaries. One night during the conference week is designated as young people's night and King's Teens Clubs come to the meeting in a group. Young people's societies from churches also come and of course our own school children. This night in the week is always a very fruitful time with many of these boys and girls finding the Lord as their Savior.

Each morning during the week, students from our schools are brought over to the tent for one of the sessions. One year a real revival broke out among our high school young people. Many lives were cleansed and purified, which made a big difference in the spiritual life of our school.

A Bible school which met twice a week was also started by the missions department, for many people were interested in attending such a school. Many of our own workers availed themselves of the opportunity to learn more of the Bible. Later the school grew to the point where a daytime Bible school was started, in addition to the night school. This school was named "King's Missionary Training Institute," with Mr. Lush in charge. It catered to the person who was looking towards the mission field and desiring practical training along with the Bible study. Here they were given the opportunity to receive practical training in many different vocations. These included mechanical work, printing, radio communications, teaching methods, nursing, cooking, and many other trades.

CHAPTER XIV

This Is the Lord's Doing

> *"This is the Lord's doing;*
> *it is marvelous in our eyes."*
> **Psalm 118:23**

For some years we had a 15 minute daily broadcast over one of the local radio stations. It was just a simple gospel program, with a song or two, and a message from our chaplain. The many letters which we received indicated a real acceptance of this program by our radio audience. One day Mike received a thirty-day written notice from the radio station, canceling our contract, saying they did not desire to have Christian programs on the air from then on, except on Sunday. He went to all the other stations, trying to get our program on some station, but he found this new policy was in effect with all the stations in the Seattle area. This was a blow to all of us and we finally decided to air the program on a station in another town. However, this was not very satisfactory.

One day when Mike was alone with the Lord in prayer, he told Him, "It does not seem right that the stations can take off all Christian programs like this. Lord, what do you want me to do about it?" Immediately the answer came back, "Why not ask me for a Christian radio station?" Since Mike knew absolutely nothing about radio it was fantastic to ask for such a thing. However, Mike's faith did not falter. Immediately he prayed, "Lord, give us a Christian radio station." Assurance came immediately and from then on Mike did not ask for a radio station, but over and over again he would thank God for the privilege of going into this new venture.

Mike hardly knew how to proceed, but he had an acquaintance with a radio engineer who worked for one of the local stations. He contacted him for advice. This man tipped Mike off to the fact that 630 on the dial might be available. He also told Mike $1,000 would be needed to make a survey. Mike went to his board members and asked for permission to have the survey made. The board, wishing to make sure that it was the Lord's will to apply for a station permit, told Mike if the Lord sent in $1,000 for the survey within a month, they would take that as a sign that it was the Lord's will. The $1,000 came in speedily, so Mike asked the engineer to make the survey. This was done and he started to make out the application papers for us. However, after a week or two, he contacted Mike and told him his employers were objecting to his working for someone else, and that he would have to discontinue his work for us.

As Mike brought this problem to the Lord, asking Him what to do, the Lord told him that He, Himself, would be the engineer. Mike should just take orders from Him. Mike had no knowledge of what to do or even the right terms to use, but he started and God undertook as Mike stepped out on His promise. Even though God did help him, Mike knew that he would have to know the right terms in making the application. To get these, he would take the former engineer out to lunch and ask him some questions. Then he would come home, pray much, and start working on the papers again. As the different forms were finished I would type them and help in any way I could. Finally the papers were all complete and we laid them out in our front room for sorting. There were so many papers, the room seemed to be full of them. After they were all finished, we committed them into the Lord's hands and sent them off. I can say to the glory of the Lord, there was not one mistake in that first application that went in, asking for the 630 spot on the dial.

A week or two later, a man contacted us and told us he too had applied for this same place on the dial and asked us to withdraw our application. When Mike told him we could not do that, he asked that we pay him $5,000 and he would withdraw his application. If both applications were left in it would mean that a hearing would have to be held in Washington D C, which was both time consuming and expensive. The Federal Communications Commission would hold the hearing and decide which application should receive the permit. Mike told the man that we could neither withdraw, nor could we pay him $5,000. The man said, "Then what are you going to do?"

Mike calmly told him, "This is the Lord's work. We are going to pray and the Lord will undertake. He will see that you withdraw your application."

This made the man very angry and he said. "Leave the Lord out of this. He has nothing to do with it." He was very upset when he left, but within a week or two he had withdrawn his application.

It took over a year for our permit to come through and during this time of waiting Mike asked for contributions for the radio station. This money was put into a separate fund and in event we did not get the permit, the money would be returned to the donors. This was not lack of faith, but he did not wish to appear to be getting money under false pretenses.

It was a happy day when a telegram arrived from Washington DC, saying we had been granted a permit for a 1,000 watt Christian radio station at 630 on the dial. One organization contacted Mike as soon as they heard we had the permit and offered to give King's Garden $5,000 if we would not exercise the permit. Mike was told by another person that this spot was worth $50,000 just for the permit alone, without a station building or equipment.

When the news that we had the permit became known, a man contacted us about a radio tower which he had in Oregon, which he desired to sell. He sold it to us at a reasonable amount of money, then said that he would further reduce the price of the tower by $1,000 if we would pay for it in full by December 20. All of the money did not come in by that date, but the man was very gracious and gave us an extension of time, which we were able to meet.

The engineer had advised that the tower should be put up near the Nightingale Building, which was higher ground, and would send out a more clear signal. However, Mike seemed to get direction from the Lord that it should be placed in the Garden of Prayer. Even though he could not understand the reason for this he was confident he had heard correctly from the Lord. The altitude of the Garden of Prayer was much lower, but he decided the tower would have to be erected there. Later the reason for this was revealed, for the lease for the Garden of Prayer part of King's Garden would not have been renewed if our radio tower had not been installed there.

To keep the cost of construction as low as possible, it was decided to put the transmitter into what had been the fire station at old Firland. This was a small building and provided cramped quarters. However, we decided it could be used for a few years until it was possible to build a new station. The play on words intrigued Mike, that the radio station was in the fire station and the signal going out from the Garden of Prayer. He would often mention that with that combination, the message going out should be warm.

We asked for and received the call letters KGDN, standing for King's Garden. Many incidents happened which continued to show our leaders that we were in the Lord's will in having this station. Some radio equipment was ordered from a company and the impression was received that $1,900 was the down-payment. When the salesman came they learned it was necessary to have $2,200 for the down-payment. Mike told the man, "We do not have all of this money and it will be necessary to pray for the funds before giving you the order." Mike and the radio leaders went into another room to pray and the assurance came that God had heard. The salesman was told, "We will have the needed money on Wednesday, and at that time we will place the order."

The money came in and the order was placed, right on time.

For some reason known only to God, the month of November was greatly used in Mike's life. It was in the month of November that:

- we were married.
- he found the Lord as his Savior.
- he surrendered completely to the Lord.
- King's Teens was started in our own home.
- the lease was signed for King's Garden.
- the quit-claim deed was signed for the Vancouver Boys' Academy.
- the Astoria Girls' School deed was signed.
- Once again, it was November when the radio station KGDN went on the air.

November 14, 1954, was a dark and gloomy day with a hint of rain. We had prayed and were confident God would keep the rain away on this Sunday afternoon. However, God did not answer this prayer by giving dry weather and those who came to see the station go on the air received a drenching, for we did not have an auditorium large enough to hold the crowds who came.

The Christian programming over KGDN was a blessing from the very beginning of the station. A great number of letters were received telling us what this station meant to them. People's hearts were blessed and numbers found the Lord as their Savior. One outstanding example was a woman who intended to commit suicide. In her distress she turned on the radio one morning and through chance she found our station. No, it was not chance for we know the Lord guided her hand to turn to the right place. She heard a talk on what God can do if He is given the chance. She immediately asked her husband to bring her to King's Garden which he did. She was ushered into Mike's office and in there on her knees she gave her heart to the Lord. Her life was completely transformed and she found something to live for.

The programs were especially comforting to those who were ill, or who were going through a trial. Others were drawn closer to the Lord when they started listening to KGDN. One woman told Mike that it had completely changed her family. They had been Christians for years, but when the children grew older they would go through the house singing the latest rock 'n roll songs, and their faith grew cold. Now she reported the children were singing the songs they heard over KGDN. Her husband had been convicted because he was not serving the Lord and now he was going to enter seminary training. Mike was especially touched one day after a meeting, when a blind woman took him by the hand and told him of what the Christian programs meant in her life, for she could not see to read her Bible.

After we went on the air a local radio station brought suit against the King's Garden, because of the similarity with their name. They won this suit in court and this restriction was a real trial to us, but gradually through the years, the restrictions were somewhat relaxed in this regard. Not only was the radio station a blessing to our radio audience and a wonderful means of getting the gospel out, but also it was a tremendous contact for the

Garden. It helped to make the King's Garden well known in the whole northwest area. Mike had a program called "Guide to Giving" on which he asked for money not only for the work of King's Garden, but also for many other worthy Christian endeavors. For some time God had been dealing with his heart about asking people for money. His theory was that there are three scriptural ways of financing the Lord's work:

1. To use one's earnings or possessions.
2. To ask others to help and pray.
3. To ask no one but God.

There is a fourth way and that is, to ask people to pray for the financial need. Mike felt this oblique way was not exactly right, for he felt those asking people to pray were hoping they would give too. He felt the more honest way was to ask for the money which was needed.

Mike felt God had asked him to use the second method. While God was dealing with him on this, Mike asked the Lord to give him a sign that he was in His will in asking for money. He was receiving criticism from many people for they thought we should operate as George Mueller did, asking only God for the money he needed. Mike told the Lord that he would go to five men and ask them for money. If this method was His will, then the men would accept his coming in the right way and that he would receive money from them.

Mike chose five men and called on them, telling them frankly about his mission. Each man gave him money and thanked him for coming. The last man on his list gave him $500 and told Mike that he hoped this would be an encouragement for him to keep asking. His words were, "How will we know where to give unless someone tells us?"

From then on Mike was not ashamed to ask for money, both by broadcasting over the radio station and by personal contact. He also began to encourage people to make out their wills and offered to help any who desired his help in this regard. Mike always felt that people should remember the Lord's work in their wills. Often Mike would take me with him when he went to call on those who had asked for help in making out their wills. It was interesting work to take down the terms of the wills in shorthand and later to type out the wills.

After our station was well established, many people began to write in saying how much they enjoyed our programs, but how much better it would be if our station was strong enough so that there would not be so much static. We began to pray once more that some way would be opened to increase the power of our station and also that we might be able to broadcast in the evening.

Mike began to make inquiries about the possibilities of increasing our station to 5,000 watts, fully expecting to be told it would be impossible. But to his surprise and joy, he received encouragement and new application papers were made out. This time there was a radio staff who took over the work of making out papers. We also applied for an FM station so that evening broadcasting would be possible. Both of these permits were received. However, before these new permits could be utilized it was necessary to build a larger place for the radio department. It had been difficult to carry on the work for the 1,000 watt station in the crowded quarters of the fire station and a house trailer was finally obtained to help provide more room. It was placed next to the station and was used to house some of the equipment. We knew that further expansion would be impossible without more room. A beautiful new structure was built and dedicated on February 14, 1960. A rally was held at the Civic Auditorium on Sunday afternoon and the switch, transferring the broadcast from the old fire house to the new building was pulled by Seattle's mayor.

The new tower was erected on the site originally recommended by the engineer. According to the terms of the permit we were given, there was a deadline when the station must be completed or we would lose the permit. There were delays in building the tower and as the last day before the deadline approached sections of the tower still lay on the ground. At last when the construction crew was ready to begin work after a delay, a snowstorm was forecast. The sky grew darker and darker and there was no doubt about the snow suspended in the upper atmosphere.

But again we prayed and were confident. Again God worked a miracle. A heavy snow fell—to the north, east and south of us—as far south as southern Oregon where snow is rare; and many schools in Oregon were closed because of the weather. But the heavy clouds bypassed Seattle and while it was storming elsewhere

King's Garden enjoyed bright sunshine and the erection of the tower proceeded without interruption.

There was a wonderful response from people who appreciated being able to hear Christian programs in the evening. So many people who worked in the daytime were not able to hear our station except on the weekends. Many of them wrote in telling of their appreciation. People in need of spiritual help began to contact King's Garden and this ministry grew to the point that our chaplain took over the major part of this work. People burdened with problems would seek out someone to help them and this ministry became a very fruitful one, with many people coming to know the Lord Jesus Christ as their Savior.

The same week, as we began broadcasting from the new building, the managers of ten Christian radio stations met at the King's Garden to organize a fellowship known as the Western Inspirational Network. Even as the Northwest Fellowship of Christian Schools was a means of one school helping another, the new radio fellowship felt that one radio station could be a help to another, and especially to help other Christian stations to get started. Mike had a vision of seeing Christian radio stations dotting the entire country and people traveling in their cars being able to enjoy Christian music for their entire trip.

CHAPTER XV

Shut the Lions' Mouths

"My God hath sent his angel and hath shut the lions' mouths . . ."
Daniel 6:22

Even though we had been fortunate in getting a new ten-year lease signed with the county commissioners, Mike continued to look to the Lord for a purchase. He felt that the promise, "I will give this city," meant that we would own King's Garden instead of just leasing it. He had no idea how God would work this all out, but he had faith that the purchase would some day be complete.

After the second lease was signed, the Anti-Tuberculosis League brought suit against us contending that the property was not being used for tuberculosis purposes. They were completely within their rights, for the deed stipulated that the property had to be used for tuberculosis purposes and if no longer needed for that purpose, then the property should be sold. The proceeds would be used to combat tuberculosis. We welcomed the lawsuit because we felt that through this means God would help us to buy the place. They lost the lawsuit but the judge ruled that the Anti-Tuberculosis League did have a reversionary interest. Mike went to the officers of this organization and told them we would like to buy this interest from them. When the property was put up for public bid, if we were the successful bidders then the title would be clear. They told Mike that by selling their interest to us, they could not guarantee we would be the successful bidder. His answer was that we believed God was going to perform a miracle and allow us to be the successful bidder. He told them we were willing to buy their interest with no promises from them. The price agreed upon between them was $37,500. Since we did not have this money Mike gave them $5,000 with the promise that the balance would be paid within a year.

Then he went back to the commissioners and told them what he had done. They thought he was very foolish to do such a thing when he had no assurance that we would be able to purchase King's Garden. The $37,000 would have to be paid even if we were not the successful bidders.

In November 1957 a special meeting was called. It was composed of the county commissioners, the Board of Managers of Firland, the city officials, the anti-tuberculosis officers and King's Garden. When they were all assembled the chairman of the commissioners said, "Mike, this is your meeting."

Mike immediately replied, "No, this is not my meeting. This is the Lord's meeting and I would ask permission to open the meeting with prayer." He did not wait for permission but immediately bowed his head and began to pray for God's blessing and asked Him to take charge of the meeting. Mike told me later he could feel that the Lord's presence was there and the whole situation was discussed amicably. Finally a motion was made to the effect that the old Firland property would be put up for public auction on April 14 and that the starting bid should be in excess of $100,000.

In order for the property to be sold at public auction, it would be necessary for us to be willing to have the new lease canceled. It took much faith to step out on the promise and willingly have the lease canceled. After this was done, the auction was advertised for a period of time, giving the date as of April 14, 1958.

On March 10, a public hearing was held in the county / city building. This meeting was for the purpose of giving people an opportunity to protest the sale of King's Garden. Even though the court had ordered the site to be sold, there were those who were desirous of hindering the sale. One group was especially insistent that ten acres of the grounds be reserved for a park. On March 20, King's Garden had a temporary restraining order served on it in an attempt to stop the sale. We had a special time of prayer, asking the Lord to lift this restraining order. This prayer was wonderfully answered.

During this time several people contacted us and said they were planning to bid for the property. We faced a real danger in this, for if others bid against us it would be possible for them to force the cost up high. Mike went on the air and told the people of our problem and asked them to pray much. He asked them to pray that we would not only be able to keep King's Garden, but that people would not bid against us and make the purchase price go so high it would be prohibitive for us. Mike's prayer was that as God closed the mouths of the lions so that they did not bother Daniel, that He would close the mouths of those who had indicated they were coming to the auction to bid. He also asked them to make contributions to a fund so that money would be on hand when he went down to bid. People really got under the burden of this prayer need and they enlisted the prayers of others, writing letters even to missionaries overseas and asking them to pray.

One man came out to see Mike and asked him to give him $10,000 if he would not bid against us. He intended to bid and to use the grounds for a housing project. Mike told him that was really blackmail but he denied this. Later Mike took one of the board members with him and called on this man and asked him to repeat what he had told him in his office. However, the man refused to do this and denied that he had tried to blackmail Mike. Time proved that he did not bid against us and Mike sent him an invitation to attend our victory dinner after the auction. Other people came out to see the King's Garden in order to ascertain how much they should bid for the place.

So the forces of evil were arrayed against the forces of good. Some people were for King's Garden being able to purchase the property and others were fighting to take it away from us. Before the date of the auction there was $50,000 in the purchase fund.

Three days before King's Garden was to be put up for auction, our lawyer decided to read the notice of auction once more. To his amazement he discovered that the terms of the transaction had to be in cash, not on time payments as we had expected. Actually a typist had made an error, yet the notice read, "terms: cash" and that was the way it remained. Our lawyer phoned Mike to ask him what would be best to do. Mike told him not reveal this information to anyone. Then he went on the air asking Christians to make large sums of money available at once on short-term loans. In just a few days Mike had promises of loans up to three million dollars if it was needed.

The day before the auction, on Sunday afternoon, we held a special session of prayer, asking the Lord to undertake. Still our prayer was that God would close the mouths of those who would bid against us.

The morning of the auction came and I decided to attend, even though I knew it would be a strain to be there. Many of our friends and also the Garden workers were at this meeting. Several other people were there too and we knew some of them came to bid. We knew that unless God undertook we would go down to defeat, but our faith was high. We believed God would take care of our problem.

It was a dramatic moment when the auctioneer read the terms of the sale: "It will be cash and the minimum bid must be in excess of $100,000." This was a blow to the people who intended to bid and who did not have enough money to pay cash in the full amount. One woman sitting next to me stiffened and muttered an unkind remark. I could tell she had intended to make a bid, but now could not do so. How wonderfully God answered prayer and closed the mouths of those who would bid against us. He did this by having a typist make a mistake.

Then the auctioneer called out, "How much am I bid?"

For a moment all was silence. Then Mike shouted, "I bid $100,001!" He had his Bible in his hand and his finger was on the promise in Jeremiah.

The auctioneer waited and then gave out the words with which this book began, "Going once, going twice . . . Is no one else going to bid? Sold to the King's Garden for $100,001."

Perhaps it would be interesting for you to read what the newspaper account had to say about his auction:

"In an auction sale climaxed by religious fervor, the old 42 acre Firland Sanatorium tract at Richmond Highlands was sold Monday to King's Garden for $100,001. The starting bid had to be $100,000—the appraised price. King's Garden bought the property for just $1 more than that. There were a few moments of breathless silence after Martin had made his successful bid. It seemed for a time that the 200 supporters of the religious organization who were present could hardly realize they had obtained the property without opposition. Then one of the workers raised his voice in the hymn, 'We'll Give the Glory to Jesus.' The audience joined in instantly and the words of the hymn rolled through the vaulted marble-walled room as impressively as in a cathedral. This hymn was followed just as enthusiastically by 'Praise God From Whom All Blessings Flow.'"

Many of the people were singing with tears streaming down their cheeks. This was certainly the high point in Mike's life to see the culmination of the years of effort.

After the excitement had died down somewhat, Mike gave a check for $40,000 with the promise the rest would be forthcoming in two or three days. When they asked him where the rest of the $100,001 was coming from, Mike remarked, "The Lord will find it for us." The rest of the money was borrowed from those who had indicated earlier they were willing to loan money. Also we owed $32,500 still, on the money we had promised to pay the Anti-Tuberculosis League. However, when people heard that we had actually secured King's Garden by purchase, contributions began to come in for this purpose.

On May 5, a victory banquet was held at the Civic Auditorium celebrating the acquisition of King's Garden. We wanted to show our appreciation to all who had helped in various ways in our securing this property. The theme of this banquet was "God Has Given the City." It was a wonderful time of rejoicing and thanksgiving to God for all He had done.

It was not until May 23, 1959, that all of the money was complete for paying off these two indebtednesses— the loans for $50,000 and the $32,5000 which we still owed to the Anti-Tuberculosis League. Theirs was the last money which we owed and the note was burned at a meeting on May 23, which happened to be Mike's birthday. He felt this was the nicest gift which he could have received.

CHAPTER XVI

Preach the Gospel

". . . Go ye ino all the world, and preach
the gospel to every creature."
Mark 16:15

In 1956, when our daughter and her husband indicated to us that they were going to New Guinea as missionaries, it was necessary for me to ask the Lord to help me. It was hard for me to see my daughter go so far away. At that time He gave me two promises: the first one was, "In losing your daughter, you will keep her," and the other was the promise that Mike and I would be able to visit them on the field. I found the first promise was fulfilled in sending packages to the family and in the letters we received from Joyce. She grew very close to me in those days through this correspondence and in my prayer for them. (Her letters were published in the book, *Dear Mom,* by Moody Press.)

I wondered how the Lord was going to work out the second promise. I had no idea, but the promise was so real to me I told everyone I came in contact with that we were going to take a trip to New Guinea. God also gave me the 91st Psalm as a promise that He would protect them on the field. When I told Mike about the 91st Psalm, he exclaimed, "I just got that from the Lord too."

After the purchase of King's Garden and all the excitement with it had died down, Mike was very weary.

He had put in ten hard years in acquiring King's Garden and he longed to get away and have a complete change. It was then we began to think about taking a trip overseas. We had no money for such a trip, but we knew if we had God's permission to go that He would provide the money. The necessary funds were provided in many different ways. In those days, after a worker had been at the King's Garden for five years, he was entitled to a three month furlough. A certain sum of money was paid into a fund each month—half paid by the worker and half by the administration. This money was available to the worker when his furlough time arrived. Mike had been so busy he could not be spared to take a long vacation when our five years were up, so it was nine years before he could think of taking his time away from the Garden. That money along with gifts from people who desired to have us make the trip, made it possible for us to go.

We left Seattle on September 12, 1958, and spent five months visiting the various mission fields. The missionaries were all so good to us and we enjoyed seeing them at work at their various endeavors. It gave us an insight into missionary life which we could have gotten in no other way. For instance, we had not realized before that missionary work is practically the same work as it is on the home field. There are church services, Sunday schools, printing presses printing the gospel, operating Bible schools, and practically everything that is done to further the cause of Christ at home, is done on the field. It made us realize as never before that the world is the field and we must determine where God wants us to labor in His vineyard.

It was all so interesting and we visited many different places—Japan, Korea, Formosa, the Philippines, Hong Kong, Dutch New Guinea, Australia, and Hawaii. We saw such needs—physical needs beyond description—but the greatest need was the spiritual one. Such great numbers of people were in need of a Savior.

Of all the fields we visited, the interior of Dutch New Guinea was by far the most primitive one. We were a little frightened by native people who wore no clothes, who never took a bath, but instead smeared their bodies with pig grease and painted their faces with clay in different colors. We were warned about being outside at night for the missionaries told us the natives thought nothing of shooting an arrow at anyone they happened to see. We viewed the missionaries with admiration for living so courageously in very adverse and dangerous conditions in order to give the Gospel to these people.

In December we came into the Territory of Papua to visit our daughter and her family over Christmas. We also had a new grandson to see, now about six weeks old. After leaving New Guinea we spent one week in Australia and one week in Honolulu and then flew home just in time to attend the King's Teens banquet in February. We both had enjoyed our trip so much and I am indeed grateful God allowed Mike to have such a trip before taking him home to be with Himself.

Shortly after returning home, on May 23, the last note was burned and King's Garden was all paid for. Then Mike began to speak of "ten years of establishment." That phrase was often on his lips and he worked diligently to establish King's Garden on a sound basis, both financially and spiritually. However, God only intended for Mike to acquire King's Garden and the establishing of the organization was to be left for others.

When Mike first received his call into the Lord's service, he told me he felt God had told him he had ten years to do the work God wanted him to do. However, as time went on and the tenth year went by since he had received his call, Mike gradually forgot about the ten years of God's promise. However, it was in the year, 1948 that God asked Mike to start a home for boys and girls from broken homes. He suffered his first heart attack at the start of 1948 and it was spring before he was well enough for us to start looking for the place of God's choice to start this home. As you know of course, it was the King's Garden God had in mind for us. One day realization came to me that it was in April, 1958, when King's Garden was purchased and that it was just ten years. Mike had done the work of acquiring King's Garden by purchase in just ten years. However, I do not believe Mike ever realized this. How faithful God has always been in keeping His promises even to the smallest detail.

CHAPTER XVII

Enter Thou Into the Joy of the Lord

"His Lord said unto him, well done,
thou good and faithful servant . . .
enter thou into the joy of thy Lord."
Matthew 25:21

Early in the spring of 1961, Mike began to talk of taking a trip to the east coast. He had some business to attend to there and he thought we might combine the business trip with our vacation. His sister Doris and her husband, Jack Geer, would go with us and we would be driving. For some unknown reason, I was very reluctant to go and seemed to have a check from the Lord. Usually, traveling was my great delight and I was always ready for a trip. I could not understand this reluctance to go, but finally it became so strong that I told Mike one evening I didn't feel I wanted to take the trip; that I had a distinct check in even thinking about going.

I asked him if he would not consider just flying to the east, conducting his business and flying home again. In that way we could take our vacation in a place where we could have some rest instead of such strenuous traveling. He thought about it for awhile and then told me he would not insist that I go, but he felt so strongly he should go that he would go alone with his sister and her husband. I told him in that case if he insisted on going on the trip I should go too, even though I had this distinct check about going. I went to the Lord in prayer and told Him that since I knew as Mike's wife I should submit my will to his, I would go. However, I was not happy about the matter and faced the trip with much apprehension.

At this time, King's Garden was steadily growing. Each department was expanding in many ways. Buoyville which had just been given to King's Garden with money enough to start building was being readied for the work of taking in boys who needed a home. Workers had been moved to the farm to get it into production. A long range program had been worked out in regard to buildings for this farm.

Many people had evidenced an interest in living in our Rest Home, but they desired to have a separate apartment to live in. For this reason, The King's Crest Apartments, with 24 units, were being built. These were just in the process of construction at the time we left for the east.

The great need in the school was for an auditorium/gymnasium and Mike had been thinking of how a building of this kind could be financed. It was still in the planning stage when Mike left, but he had told me he thought he would start pressing towards beginning to build in the fall. This structure could serve a dual purpose and be used for large gatherings. He especially had in mind the missionary conference, which was held in the spring of each year. It was necessary to erect a tent each year to house the conference and to have a large auditorium would be a great advantage.

Outside painting of all the buildings on the grounds had been started. Plans were being made to make the grounds more beautiful, with new lawns replacing the old worn out ones and new shrubs and flowers being planted. Mike was working towards stabilizing every phase of the work, and revising the organizational set up. The apartment we had lived in when we first moved to King's Garden had been remodeled and made into an executive wing, with offices for Mike and for his assistant, his brother Vernon. The sitting room was turned into a place for the King's Garden board to hold their meetings. Mike had occupied his new office only two weeks before we left on our trip.

We left on June 4 and for the first week we had a very enjoyable time. Then we reached Chicago where we had rooms reserved for us at the Evangelical Alliance Mission. On Sunday morning we went to Moody Church and during the service Mike sneezed several times. He often had attacks of hay fever and we just laughed, thinking something in the church had caused his hay fever to come to the fore. However, by evening it was apparent it was not hay fever, but a cold coming on. We got some medicine for him at the drug store and went on to Wheaton where Mike had a service that evening. He said nothing, but I believe Mike was feeling quite ill after the service and insisted that we stay at Wheaton College all night instead of going back to our rooms at TEAM Headquarters. The next morning the three of them went sight-seeing while I stopped at a laundromat to do some needed washing. After lunch we drove back to Chicago and the two men went out to see Moody Press. Mike left his manuscript for the book, *I Live By Faith* with them and asked if they would check to see if it was something which would be good to publish. Doris and I went shopping and later met the men. Then we went to friends for dinner.

The next morning we were going to get an early start for Detroit. Mike was going to drive first. Before leaving Chicago, he drove into a gas station. While the attendant was filling the tank, Mike came to the car and told us. "I have a severe pain in my chest and perhaps before I leave town I should see a doctor." So we drove back to TEAM Headquarters, obtained the name of a doctor, and drove over to his office. The doctor made arrangements for Mike to have laboratory tests that afternoon and told him to go to his room and rest until that time. He gave him some pills to help kill the pain.

We went back to our room and Mike had a good nap until noon. When he woke up he said he felt normal once more and wanted to continue our trip. It was so terribly warm in Chicago and he felt if we could reach Detroit it might be cooler. The four of us knelt and prayed. We all received the same answer that we should continue on to Detroit before Mike received a complete check-up. Mike stood the trip very well, even eating a good meal in a restaurant that evening. We reached Detroit about ten and immediately went to the home of the Fred Renichs, former missionaries, where we were to stay. Mike undressed and got into bed and then told us he felt hungry. A bowl of hot soup was soon forthcoming and he seemed to enjoy it a great deal. After eating he leaned back and murmured, "That was good."

Immediately the pain came back again and he was in agony in just a few seconds. Renichs called a doctor who lived nearby and by midnight Mike was in the hospital. Because of the crowded conditions, it was necessary to keep him in the out-patient clinic over night. I sat with him all that long night, only leaving him long enough to call my children in Seattle. Doctors and nurses came and went all night long, ministering to him. I was told he had suffered a major heart attack complicated by pneumonia.

In the morning he was moved into a room. He seemed to be brighter. He began to make gains in a real fight for his life. I knew much prayer was going up to the Throne of Grace in his behalf and I was confident he was going to get well. I stayed with him at the hospital during the day, going back to the Renichs to sleep. He was able to talk with me for a few minutes at a time and then he would sleep for awhile. He mentioned several times how thankful he was that we had gone on to Detroit, for the weather was so much cooler.

Sunday morning when I reached the hospital, Mike began to tell me of a dream he had had the night before. He said he had dreamed he had gone to heaven. Heaven was not a bit as he thought it was, but it was composed of different stations, for different groups of people. The higher stations were for those who were the more yielded Christians. Mike and I had often talked of what heaven was like and we had come to the conclusion the new Jerusalem must be a mountain, for the Bible says it is 1,500 miles high and has one street of gold. We thought perhaps the street wound round and round until it reached the bottom of the mountain.

As he told me of his dream, I laughingly said, "I suppose you went to the foot of the mountain." He looked so bashful for a minute and then nodded his head and said nothing. I went on, "Then the Lord came and took you up higher, didn't He?"

He said softly, "That was just what happened." He paused as if reluctant to appear to be bragging, and then said, "He took me up quite a ways. I think I know what heaven is like now." I wanted to talk more to him about the matter, but the doctor had said he must keep his mind fixed on the fact that he wanted to get well. I was afraid that if his mind dwelt too much on heaven, he would lose his desire to live. For that reason, I changed the subject and began to talk to him about how much we needed him and he must do all he could to get well once more.

Since he was making progress, Jack and Doris Geer decided to take the car and travel on. Jack would attempt to conduct the business for Mike. By Tuesday morning Mike was so much better that he was taken out of the oxygen tent and his pneumonia jacket came off. He was told he could have a shave, so I called in a barber. Then he wanted me to comb his hair and he insisted that it be parted just right. The man in the next bed laughed and told Mike he was giving me an impossible task when he had so little hair. He was so relaxed and happy that day and we had a good time talking together about what we were going to do in the future. Once he said, "The Lord seems to have set the stage for something and I don't know just what it is."

I leaned over his bed and said, "Do you see now why I didn't want to take this trip?"

A wide grin was his only answer.

Towards evening he began to be weary so I told him I would go down to the cafeteria for a cup of coffee and then go on home. After drinking my coffee, I went back to his room but he was sound asleep. I did not bother him, but just took my purse and left. The next morning Mr. Renich awakened me at 6:00 A.M. and told me Mike had gone to be with the Lord. As far as the nurse could ascertain, he had slipped away in his sleep. It was hard to understand for he had been doing so well. As I stood in my room at the Renichs, bewildered and shocked, the Lord spoke so definitely, "Can you praise Me now?"

I had to be honest and say, "No, Lord, I can't praise You for this." It took a few days before I could thank the Lord for taking Mike from me.

I called Seattle and told them the sad news. The children asked that I come home immediately. There was a plane at 10:00 A.M. and we had quite a race in order for me to get to the airport in time. Before I could go, it was necessary to make arrangements for a funeral home to take charge of Mike's body, and we hurried much to get everything done. I am indeed indebted to the Renichs for their kindness to me in my time of need.

When I reached Chicago, I found that the plane for Seattle was delayed and I would have a three hour wait. As I turned away from the counter after receiving this information, I really felt God had deserted me. How could I fill up three hours when I was so numb with pain. I still had not shed any tears, but this long wait was almost more than I could bear.

Realizing I had had nothing to eat that morning, I went into the lunch counter and had a bowl of soup and some coffee. I came back to the waiting room and reasoned with myself this way! I would sit on a bench for ten minutes, then I would get up and walk for ten minutes, then repeat the process over and over. Perhaps in that way time would pass.

I got up to start walking and saw my youngest son coming towards me. I was so bewildered at seeing him, I was dazed. We grabbed each other and both of us began to cry. Oblivious to those around us, we wept our way to composure once more. Then we began to compare notes on how he happened to be in the Chicago airport.

He had received the message of his father's death while at a conference in Minneapolis. He was told which plane I was on and he decided to attempt to reach me in Chicago if he could. His plane in from Minneapolis landed on the other side of Chicago. To get to me involved a ride in a helicopter over the city. Now he was there to comfort me in my time of need, and I felt ashamed of myself for feeling God had deserted me. He knew of my need and had arranged a few miracles so that Michael could meet me and be with me for the rest of the journey.

Mike's funeral was held in the First Presbyterian Church in Seattle, to accommodate all who wished to come for the memorial service. Rev. Melvin Dahlstrom, who had been our pastor some years before, gave the message. Hilding Halvarson sang two songs which had meant much in Mike's life—"God Is Waiting" and "For I Have Decided to Follow Jesus." Bob and Elizabeth Staley sang "Blessed Assurance," which had for years been Mike's testimony. It was a sweet service and my heart was completely at peace. I did not even feel like weeping for I knew Mike was at home with the Lord whom he loved so much. If he had lived he might have been an invalid and I know how he would have hated that. Mike was always so full of life and interested in people.

Two weeks before we left on our trip, he talked with my oldest son, Curtis, and told him if anything happened to him, he wanted him to be the one to handle my affairs and watch out for me. It would almost seem that Mike had a premonition that he was soon to go to be with the Lord.

In the spring a cemetery manager came to Mike and offered to give him two cemetery plots as a gift, for both of us. Mike's response to this gift was something like this, "I had hoped to be taken up in the rapture, but God never gives me anything which I cannot use, so I accept this gift gratefully." On Memorial Day we went out with our youngest son and his wife, to see the lots. They were located in such beautiful surroundings near a fountain, and as we stood gazing at them Mike turned to Kathy. He said, "Kathy, this is where I am going to be. Will you put flowers on my grave?" Only a few weeks later his body was there, but Mike was at home with the Lord.

Accomplished By Faith

When my three children and I began to compare notes, we were amazed when we realized all of the many things which had happened to indicate that Mike was unconsciously being prepared for his homegoing. My daughter and her family had endeavored to return to the field that spring and had been told definitely there were no reservations available on any boat until fall. If they had managed to find a boat that was leaving they would have been on the ocean when Mike left us. Instead all three of the children were there together in Seattle and only our foster daughter and her family needed to come from a distance.

At the King's Garden board meeting held a month before we left on our trip, Mike began to speak of what could happen to me if he should die. At first the members were rather jovial about Mike being concerned about dying, but when they saw he was very serious, they told him if he preceded me in death, they would see that I was cared for, for the rest of my life. They asked him to write into the minutes of the meeting just what he wanted. Later Mike dictated to me what he wanted written into the minutes and he was very specific as to what he wanted for me in case he should die.

A week after the funeral I returned to our home and endeavored to get all of our things packed away. There were also many of Mike's papers to go through. Michael and Kathy came to stay with me during this time, until I could make plans to move. One of the things which touched me deeply was a letter from Moody Press, accepting the manuscript of Mike's book, *I Live By Faith*.

The letter was written two days before Mike's death, without their knowing he was even ill.

I felt the need of getting away from the King's Garden and all of the memories there. I especially missed Mike in the evenings for it was then we would walk around the grounds, visiting with those we met. We would inspect any new project which was underway and so often he would tell me how much he loved the Garden. He marveled that God had chosen him to start such a large work.

When Rod and Joyce asked me to return to New Guinea with them in October I was glad to accept. The change was of great benefit. So this book has been written thousands of miles from home.

I am grateful to God for the 35 years of married life which Mike and I enjoyed together. I knew his heart was weak and that he would probably go to heaven ahead of me. Mike often would say that we were more than husband and wife; that we were friends as well. We could talk happily together on many topics for long periods of time. Though we are now separated, I know I will see Mike again. What a comfort this is in my present loneliness.

Thank you for your interest in these inspiring books by Mike and Vivian Martin. It is our hope that they have been a blessing to you. If you would like more information about this book or the work currently being done by CRISTA Ministries, contact:

CRISTA Ministries
19303 Fremont Avenue North
Seattle, Washington 98133